LET'S GO PLAY IN THE BOMB BUILDINGS:

A WELSH GIRLHOOD

Thelma Wheatley

First published 2024
by Rowanvale Books Ltd
The Gate
Keppoch Street
Roath
Cardiff
CF24 3JW
www.rowanvalebooks.com

A CIP catalogue record for this book is available from the British Library.
ISBN: 978-1-83584-013-9
e-Book ISBN: 978-1-83584-014-6

To Lorna,
In loving memory,
And to Peter Wheatley, fondly.

TABLE OF CONTENTS

So all day long the noise of battle roll'd
Among the mountains by the winter sea

—Morte d'Arthur, Tennyson.

PREFACE:

THE SILENT GENERATION

My twin sister, older brother and I were part of what is now called the "Silent Generation", born between the mid-1930s and 1945 after World War II. We were deemed quiet, conservative and conforming, on the outside at least, in contrast to the self-expressive, individualistic, noisy, rebellious "Hippie" generation that followed with their long hair, beads and guitars. We girls had short, neat hair and often wore brooches on our left shoulders. We did as we were told. We did not answer back. We ate everything put in front of us on our plates. We knew the Lord's Prayer and the multiplication tables to twelve-times-twelve by age six, and did mental arithmetic. Of course, there were no calculators, TV, computers, cell phones or even phones then. Only the local doctor had the luxury of a telephone.

We were expected to walk to school alone even as young as age five, often a mile or more, and deal with whatever bullying came up. Sometimes we became the bullies ourselves, a phenomenon blamed on "the War" we'd all just come through. Some girls carried pen-knives and toy swords stuck into their belts. (I had a home-made wooden sword of my own that I secretly brandished about with an idea of being Sir Galahad.) We caught buses and the Mumbles electric train as needed, and kept our fares in our pockets. We were resourceful. We were hard-working and loyal, and got jobs right after school ended and saved our money. We loved our neighbours and looked after our parents in their old age, when possible. The teachers beat and fisted us in school and we did not protest, nor did our parents. We understood they were not on our side.

But our humble, hard-working parents who had fought in the Wars gave us one wonderful gift: they allowed us total freedom to play outside unsupervised in the streets, the bomb shelters, down the woods and fields and seashore. Those glorious hours in the fresh air, boys and girls together of all ages, filled with joy and games, teasing and taunting, playing kissing games and other adventurous sexual proclivities that might shock – even horrify – the "helicopter" parents of today. The unspoken rule being we kept our doings to ourselves, secret from the adults – and they never asked; as long as we were home for tea by four o'clock.

LET'S GO PLAY IN THE BOMB
BUILDINGS

It seemed Drusilla and I had fallen asleep again on the pavement outside. "Those poor little twins, just lying there," the neighbours rumbled.

Mrs Walsh from number 7 came and shook us awake and went and knocked on the door. "Mrs Thomas, yewer twins is fallen asleep by the road, they're gonna get run over one of these days." And she pointed at us from the doorway.

Mammy was smoking – at least cigarettes weren't rationed. "Oh-h?" she answered vaguely, as if what was she supposed to do about it? It was summertime and hot and kids do fall asleep in the sun.

She gave us a bowl of bread and milk, powdered milk out of a tin that you mixed with water. Davey got an egg as well because he was a boy and was nine turning ten, and that was fair; we were only four. We got half an egg each because we were twins, and that was fair too. Was it any wonder I failed logic at university?

Each morning, Mammy gave us a teaspoon of thick, dark orange juice to swallow, like syrup, to prevent scurvy, and a teaspoon of cod liver oil to fight everything else, supplied for free by the Labour government for Britain's children. They came in opaque brown bottles. "Open your mouths." We were obedient children.

Our brother David, whom we called Davey for short, had a giant catapult. He belonged to the Powys gang of boys that went around shooting at kids who dared venture on our street from other streets, and people's pigeons and occasional passing cars. Sometimes they found burnt-out shells from the Blitz in the bombed buildings. Davey wore short thick trousers with little buttons up the fly, long ribbed British woollen socks to his knees, a V-necked sleeveless jersey over his shirt, and his school cap with a badge on the front. We wore homemade dresses that Mammy sewed on a second-hand Singer sewing machine she inherited from Nanny, using material she bought from the drapery stall in what used to be Swansea Market. She'd used up the last of her clothing coupons for the dresses. There was rationing for everything: food, clothes, petrol for Daddy's motorbike. "Oh I *long* for butter!" Mammy would sigh mysteriously; we had no idea what she meant. "*Hate* margarine!" Another cypher we were supposed to comprehend. Margarine was twice as cheap as butter in the ration book. The ration book from the Ministry of Food bore Mammy's name, Mavis Thomas, her address, when she was born (1912) and serial number. It was the most important thing on earth and Mammy was not to lose it. She took it with her shopping at the market, and Nanny Norman had one too. "You can't even get buried these days without a ruddy stamp for your coffin," she said.

But we were alive. Daddy once called us "war babies" and "lucky ter be alive". People said things like that: "If your name's on the bomb you'll get it." A whole street would be blown to bits by the Luftwaffe and one house left standing, untouched, Nanny liked to say over a cup of tea with her neighbour, stressing *untouched*.

"Lower Goat Street, bombed," she informed her friend, Elvira Perman, one morning – "Mrs Perman" to us. Nanny lived in the centre of Swansea town, the worst place to be in an air raid, in a tall gloomy house. It was in the Sandfields, so called because when the sea rose at high tide during a storm, everyone had to put out rows of sandbags provided by the town council to create a barrage; the area was below sea level, something I couldn't understand. Would the sea roll in over poor Nanny at night? Nanny shook her head at the memory, but really, lugging out sandbags to make a barricade in front of the house, and the appearance of men to help her who hadn't been called up, made it exciting.

"What with that and them flying incendiary bombs, what was next?" She spoke in an ironic tone.

Drusilla and I sat without a murmur on the settee in the middle room until Mammy came back from shopping; we were not allowed to take part in adult conversation, something we were born knowing. We were sucking on half a stick of rock each that Nanny had saved for us from her trip to Blackpool to visit her sister. I was holding mine reverently. Suddenly, quick as a whip, Drusilla snatched it out of my hand and licked it all over with her tongue up and down, soaking it with her horrible spittle. Of course I couldn't suck it after that and I realised then that Drusilla had somehow known that, that was her power over me, and so she got two halves to herself and Nanny never even noticed. Drusilla gave me a smirk that said everything, my whole future. I knew then I was helpless to protect myself against something for which there were no words.

"Well we survived it, touch wood!" said Mrs Perman, tapping her head as a joke. She was a tiny woman with frizzy, dyed red hair like a wig, and sharp, blue eyes. "Yewer eyes will fall out of yewer 'ead, one day, Miss Kezia Thomas," she suddenly said of me. "Listens in to everything, that one, don't she, Emmie, not like the other one."

That was how people talked about us twins: "this one" and "that one", as if Drusilla and I were a couple of potatoes, one with black eyes in it and one without.

"Yes, we was lucky, Elvira," Nanny agreed. They were talking of the three-day blitz on Swansea, 19 to 21 February, 1941, before Drusilla and I were actually born. We were "on the way", said Nanny.

"All them incendiaries – 'ow many were there?" Thousands, and that was just the first night.

"Thirty thousand incenjaries, not to mention 'igh explosives," said Mrs Perman gloomily. "Five thousand bombs. Teilo Crescent in Mayhill got it the worst, *demolished,* and sixty-one butchers in town – *gorn.*"

"I was down in the cellar on my knees in the dark saying the Lord's Prayer. 'Please God, dun' let the Luftwaffe get me,'" said Nanny.

Drusilla and I listened wide-eyed, it sounded desperate.

"Right you are, Emmie, we would 'ave been done for but for Him." Mrs Perman nodded, pointing to the ceiling. "And 'ow is Mavis doing? She got a lot on 'er plate." Meaning us twins.

"Aye, well she got married at eighteen and 'ad Davey, and then the war come along and bango, *twins.*" We sounded like a disaster. "An' she's so thin, arms like sticks from the rationing."

Nanny got out the last of her sherry from the Welsh dresser. She'd been keeping it to buck herself up in emergencies, such as attacks by Hitler's Luftwaffe. "I says to her at the time, 'Well, Mavis, you made your bed now lie on it.' Fancy a nip?"

"Just a nip, Emmie, thank you."

It was all Nanny had left. I understood everything had to be for *them*, "our boys", the soldiers "over there" (somewhere): all the meat, ham, sugar, butter, eggs, you name it, gladly sacrificed by Nanny and Mrs Perman.

Everybody had the feeling of being spared after the all clear. "Somebody wuz looking out for us," we heard people say. "Still walking around." Tottering houses smouldering, windows blasted; craters where Ben Evans department store had once been on Oxford Street. Dark holes, jagged glass. And the worst was Swansea Market with its beautiful arches and glass vault that had shone like translucent angel wings over the mean little stalls of faggots and cockles and second-hand clothes below. Shattered. Just shattered; glass splinters of light hanging in the twilight. "Gone," said Nanny, and wept some tears.

"A shame," agreed Mrs Perman. She patted Nanny's bony hand. "There, dear."

Frightening, things suddenly being gone, time gone, knowing something had been there and then it wasn't, I thought. Oh, where was Mammy, and I didn't even have my piece of rock.

***

Our house was dark and dingy, of dull, dark red brick ingrained with a century of soot, like all the others on the street. Mammy complained.

"But we're lucky, Mavis, mun," said Daddy. "At least we only 'ave a neighbour on one side of us."

It was true. We had the end house in the row. On the other side was a thick privet hedge hiding the school lane; all the kids trudged up the lane before the nine o'clock bell. There was a small front garden of scraggly grass, and at the back of the house a sloping yard with wrought iron railings at the top. The railings backed on to the school and we could see its rows of peaked windows and dormers and square panes of glass from our bedroom windows. It had a gloomy entrance, one called Boys and one Girls, where you lined up at the bell.

One day, chickens appeared in the kitchen, little fluffy brown and white things running around squeaking for food, seeds that Mammy threw down. "Oh, what have I come down to in life? Now *chickens* in the house," she fretted.

"Well at least they'll have real eggs!" cried Daddy, who always looked on the bright side. "Not them powdered eggs they bin having."

Mammy brightened up too, happy at last. Daddy grinned. But we didn't like the real eggs at breakfast; we wanted the powdered eggs we were used to.

"You got to like them," said Daddy.

A real egg had a round shell and was hard. When you cracked it open with your teaspoon it was all red and gooey inside, with horrible white jelly-like stuff around it.

"Ugh-h, dun' like it," whined Drusilla, so I whined too as we were twins, and we pushed our eggs away in their little china cups.

"Wassat red thing, Mammy?"

A red spot, very suspicious, floating in Drusilla's runny yolk. "Ooh, agh."

"Good for you, mun," cried Daddy, grinning, but neither he nor Mammy would say what the spot was though they knew the answer; they sneaked a look at each other – what did it mean?

I was frightened of the house on the outside, and all the other houses up and down the street of Powys, stuck together, all with the same gloomy look. The rain swept down the pavements and dark clouds hung over the chimney pots. I was frightened inside the house, too.

A square living room with a big table, two armchairs, one each side of the fireplace. Daddy sat in the armchair and put his feet up, warming them before the flames, listening to his records. He'd put his favourite on his gramophone we weren't allowed to touch: His Master's Voice, with a picture of a white dog listening by the horn, head cocked. The voice was a man's, loud and roaring, I didn't understand the words. "Iz Italyun. Iz a naria." Then he played "Keep Right on to the End of the Road", and I knew the words because he played it so often, sung by Harry Lauder.

"Oh not that old thing again," said Mammy crossly.

The curtains were drawn against the drizzly night, and the room glowed from the fire. She wanted Ivor Novello singing "We'll Gather Lilacs in the Spring Again".

"We'll gather lilacs in the spring again,
And walk together down an English lane."

"If 'Itler don't blow them to blazes," growled Daddy.

Behind the living room was the kitchen with a window looking out over the back. There was a deep old tin sink. Off the kitchen was the mysterious bathroom, cold and narrow. The bath was deep with carved lion's legs. One afternoon, Mammy lay in the bath with no clothes on, soaking herself, her titties floating in the water.

"What's those?" I pointed to large brown circles with little pricks sticking up in the middle. Drusilla and I stared, watching Mammy soap herself with a bar of pink Puritan soap.

"Those are my teats," she smiled. "You and Drusilla used to suck them, one on each side, as babies."

But I wanted them to myself.

"Oh you're too old for that, Kezia, you're four."

Mammy heaved herself out of the water, which ran in rivulets down her legs onto the tiles. She wrapped a towel round her, suddenly irritated, Drusilla and I prancing around, excited, raising our hands. "Suck Mammy's teats!"

Mammy pushed me away especially hard. "You damn kids!" She stomped into the living room, where Davey was reading his comics by the window for light: *Morgyn the Mighty*. "I'm SICK and FED UP of you kids all day long! I'm leaving, I'm leaving if you two keep this up. Damn twins!"

Drusilla spun round in the middle of the room, her little hands – the fingers much littler than mine – raised in horror as if fending off an incendiary attack.

"No, Mammy, please no, dun' leave me, please please, I'll be good," she promised, tears running down her cheeks. She was beside herself.

I was horrified, not just at the bomb Mammy had hurled into the living room, exploding in our midst, but at Drusilla – she really believed it; she was beside herself, trying to cling to Mammy's legs. "Please please, Mammy, I'll be good, I'll be good…" I wasn't sure Mammy meant this terrible thing; surely she wouldn't leave us. Where would she go? To Nanny's, of course.

I think that was about the time I started stealing.

***

"Did you *steal* the books, Kezia Thomas, and push them down your bodice? LOOK AT ME WHEN I'M SPEAKING TO YOU. *TELL THE TRUTH.*"

"No, Miss, no I never, I never…"

Miss Ferris, headmistress of Powys Nursery School, leaned over me in her private office. (The two young assistant teachers in the playroom had marched me down the hall with the offending evidence, which they'd apparently pulled out of my chest.) Miss Ferris looked hard at me; she didn't like children. Mammy had handed us over with nary a backward glance to this grim woman in a building with double portals and long, peering windows. *Answer when you are spoken to.*

Miss Ferris had short, iron-grey hair swept back in an efficient manner, and a brusque tone. She wore a tweed suit and a shiny silk blouse underneath with a pin at the throat. I've always had a horror since for those glittering pins middle-aged women pierce through their lapels.

The steel pin loomed over me. "TELL THE TRUTH, KEZIA THOMAS. You hid them *down your bodice*."

She held out the proof, the books, which were tiny, about one and a half inches long and wide, precious, darling little things with little rabbits gambolling over the covers. I *had* to have them, not just to read, but to have them for mine, to love. (Looking out at the long, sad window in the playroom, the way sunlight fell outside…)

"No, Miss, no I never, I never, I never…" I would deny it to my dying day, my voice fading in terror before I slumped at Miss Ferris' feet on the parquet floor, with a thud.

Mammy was sent a note and had to be called up to the nursery. "Well, Mrs Thomas, of course we never imagined she would go this far and actually *faint*."

"Well, she is only just four…"

The books were given back; Mammy was vaguely on my side. "A fuss over nothing." There was something splendid about Mammy in the moment, the way she swept into the office in her homemade dress. She was not going to be intimidated by a Miss Ferris in her tweed suit with an ugly pin in its lapel; on the other hand, her precious afternoons free of us kids hung in the balance.

"The twins *love* the nursery school, Miss Ferris, and you do a wonderful job with them," she purred.

Mammy really believed it. "You and Drusilla *loved* nursery school, Kezia, you don't remember," filled me with despair. For a while after, Mammy walked us to the nursery and picked us up later, but after a week of this she tired and she got two older girls to do it, any girls. They loved to mind us.

"Which one do you want, Gwynneth?"

"Oh I thinks this one with the ringlets." Drusilla.

"Then I'll 'ave Kezia, she's the quiet one."

And they'd take off with us up the street holding our hands, Mammy had no idea where, while she did her washing. She did it in the kitchen. She got out the washing board with ribs and a bar of green wartime soap, scrubbing sheets till her hands were raw, and then she had to put them through the mangle, turning the handle; oh it was a job. She was all hot and flustered when we got back, hungry and thirsty. The girls had taken us too far, though we didn't know that. So now she had to get out some food for us from the pantry, bread and jam that she didn't have.

Once, the rent man came knocking at the door. "Quick, hide under the tablecloth, you two, and don't move." She pushed us under the long damask cover. "Don't make a noise."

The rent man kept on knocking. He carried a bag for the money and a square clipboard and a pencil stub. Mammy was in a panic and ducked down under the stairs. "Sh-sh-sh," she giggled.

The front door had a small, high, glazed window he couldn't see through, but he knew we were inside, I was sure. Eventually, he went away; we heard his footsteps echoing down the path. Mammy came out, red in the face that she didn't have any money, just like the Jenkinses down the street. I was worried, something very bad was going on here.

"Well, I'll pay next time," said Mammy. It was ten shillings and sixpence.

There were lots of kids on Powys Avenue, so it was safe to let us out to play alone by ourselves now that we were a year older; that was the reasoning. Davey was supposed to keep an eye on us as our older brother; another assumption. Children should be out in the fresh air developing their lungs and building their bones from natural sunlight. (Mammy and Daddy belonged to something called the Health and Strength League of Britain, grand words that I admired the sound of.) Mammy had steel expanders from before the war that she sometimes pulled and stretched sideways across her chest to improve her physique, then she'd collapse in the armchair and smoke a Woodbine cigarette. A few years later, when other people moved in and we moved out, I found cigarette stubs in the cupboard.

Mammy put up the regulation blackouts at our bedroom window; it was the rule so the German bombers at night couldn't see where the house was and drop a bomb on us. The room went black.

"Ooh, Mammy." Drusilla and I curled into each other, holding tight in the sinking double bed, pulling the eiderdown over our heads. We could just make out Mammy's face in the dark. "Don't go, Mammy."

"Nighty-night." She was cheerful because she was going downstairs to listen to her serial on the radio. It was a novel by someone called Galsworthy, and involved a woman's long moans floating up the stairs every Thursday evening: "*Oh-h Soames… Soames… SOAMES!*"

There was just the bed and a chest of drawers wedged against the window with its muffled blackouts. The window in the daytime looked out over the yard and the bomb shelter. Something ticked in the dark.

Davey had a room to himself, as he was a boy. It had a single bed and a small, black, lead fireplace. When he was sick, Daddy lit a fire in the grate using balls of newspaper and some lumps of anthracite he carried up from the coal-house in a bag. "Best Welsh coal in the world."

Ooh, the flames were lovely, licking the lumps. Red shadows glowed round the walls and lit up Davey's face, which was awful thin; he didn't get enough meat, I heard Nanny say to Mrs Perman. Davey lay back against the pillow, his face spotty. He had his comics spread over the counterpane, *Beano* and old *Dandy*s and his favourite, *Hotspur*.

"C'n I look too, Davey?" Drusilla and I sat on the bed side by side, looking around.

"You can't read proper."

"Ooh she can, Kezia c'n read," nodded Drusilla.

"Then read *that*. Heh! See. You dun' say *g* like that, it's like *juh*. Rojuh the Dojuh!" Roger the Dodger.

"You in Davey's room, you two?" Mammy called up the stairs. "You're not supposed to be in there, you'll catch the measles!"

***

"Let's go play in the bomb buildings!"

Excited, Drusilla and I ran out and squeezed between the railings to the bomb shelter that we all called the bomb building. That was a fun place in the schoolyard, running and screaming round and round the heavy block of concrete, creeping to the narrow entrance, being frightened, daring yourself: "I'm not afraid. Ooh, yes I am." A secret place with a dark opening, full of the echo of something. (When you called your name it rolled back from the dark, from somewhere in there, not yours, someone else's voice; whose?) How were we to know it was full of ghosts, people who had crowded in there like a tomb at dead of night with their blankets and gas masks and babies, the siren going off, a high whistling whine – *air raid!* – and Mammy screaming "Oh God! Oh God!" till the all clear. Davey knew, he knew everything; he was there.

"I know, let's play being dead," said Dulcie Jenkins. Was she malevolent, a word Nanny used, that I didn't know but felt?

Drusilla started crying. "Dun' wanna be dead, please, Dulcie."

Dulcie was with her sister Lil; they both had runny noses and dresses too tight for them. Our dresses had puff sleeves and pockets with little matching handkerchiefs Mammy sewed herself. "Well, Mrs Thomas does keep them twins lovely," people grudged. Dulcie's teeth were greenish from chewing liquorice and Spanish root. She didn't have enough to eat.

"Wanna suck?" she offered. I wiped the stick first with my hanky and took a suck. Ooh, it was sharp and spicy; then Drusilla had a suck. Dulcie watched. "Now both yewer teeth is green."

"Me 'n' Dulcie goin' up on th' roof," said Lil. The roof of the bomb building.

"C'n I come up?"

"Yew too little."

"Davey pulls me up."

Davey had his gas mask on, whizzing round the schoolyard being Dick Barton, special agent. "Wheee!" He was with his best friend Dai Lilley. They climbed up on the roof and Davey hauled me up by my arms.

Drusilla stayed on the ground. "Mammy said…"

It was lovely up there, high up. From the roof you could see everything: Mr Penry's pigeons in a coop on stilts, all the back gardens and washing lines, the schoolyard sloping as far down as the outside lavatories, one for girls, one for boys, awful smelly. But up here it was fresh and the light was different. Davey was in standard four and the boss, so in silence we stood, following his finger to where it pointed far away in the distance, past the roundabout to Mayhill – "down there" – to little dots that were the bombed houses where we also weren't supposed to play but did, following Davey and his friend. Daddy had said, "They building new 'ouses down there." But we knew better; they were the bombed buildings to play house in, and hide and seek, amongst the burnt-out shells of someone's flattened living room or kitchen, cupboard shelves teetering in splinters, cans of jam splattered across the wall where we saw mice running crazed, and then Drusilla screaming, her eyes squeezed shut. The scream went on and on. She was pointing at her feet at the torso of a doll with its head blown off in the rubble of what was left of Teilo Crescent.

***

There was no guard rail, of course, on the roof of the bomb shelter to stop you falling over the edge, a drop of ten or twelve feet where you'd smash your head at the bottom, smirked Dulcie. Mrs Penry was hanging out her washing four doors down, and we watched from up high as she went and shouted at our back door, "Mrs Thomas, yewer Kezia is up on the roof of the bomb shelter, she's gonna fall and break 'er neck."

At once, Drusilla down below started wailing, "Kezia's gonna break her neck." So Davey dropped me back down over the edge, and Dulcie and her sister jumped it by themselves as they were older. They landed with a thud but nothing hurt the Jenkinses, they were made of concrete, and they ran off.

Presently, Mammy came out into the garden, calling from the railings. Drusilla was gone inside. It was getting dark and birds were wheeling round the chimney pots.

"What're you still doing out here, Kezia? You know you're always supposed to stay with Drusilla." She looked at me suspiciously. My dress was dusty and my knees scraped, but I still had two ribbons in my hair and my hanky in my pocket, so that was all right. She hesitated, standing against the sky in her thin, sad dress, smoking as twilight fell. The war would soon be over, any day now, any day now.

Mammy had a nice face; when she smiled you lit up all inside, and you forgot everything, everything.

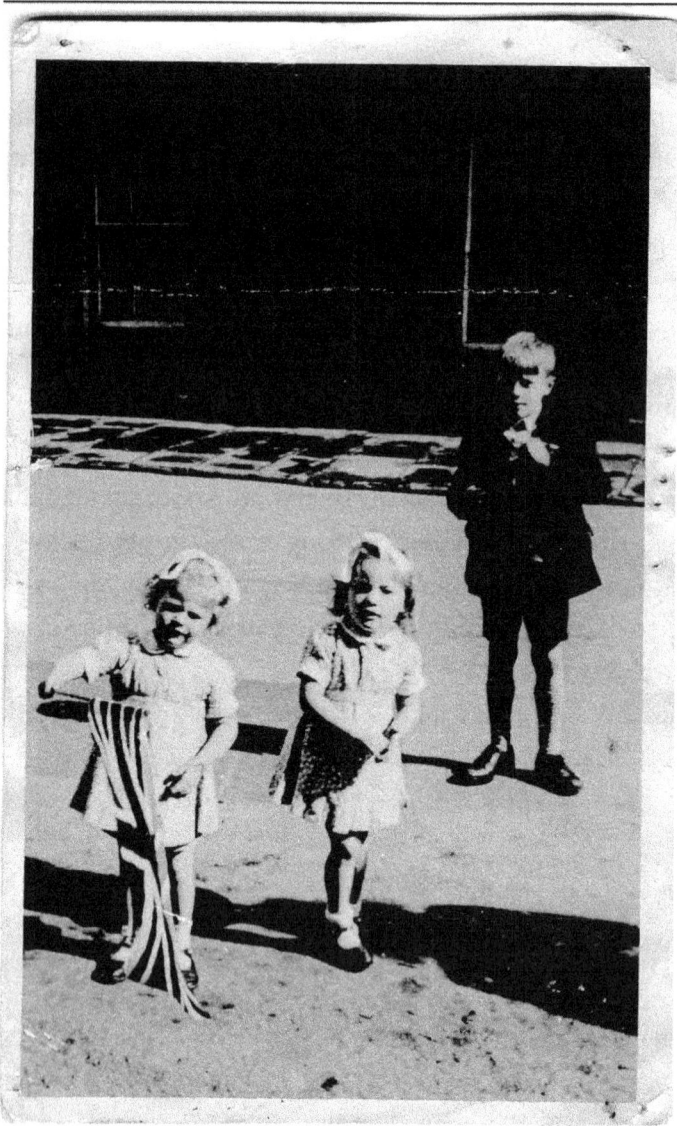

The author, her twin sister and brother on V.E. Day, the End of the War, May 8. 1945, Swansea.

SWANSEA ARCHIVES

The people of TEILO CRESCENT who lost their lives in the Blitz: 20 February 1941:

- Wilfred Barnes of 45 Teilo Crescent, aged 44.
- Bernard Roy Bija of 37 Teilo Crescent, aged 16.
- Kenneth Howard Bija of 37 Teilo Crescent, aged 15.
- John Ernest Murray Bishop, Home Guard volunteer, of 38 Teilo Crescent, aged 26.
- Timothy Buckley of 15 Teilo Crescent, aged 49.
- John Buckley of 15 Teilo Crescent, aged 14.
- Florence Kate Cratchley of 29 Teilo Crescent, aged 65.
- Josiah Cobley of 55 Teilo Crescent, aged 59.
- Brinley Joshua Cook of 39 Teilo Crescent, aged 40.
- Ernest Thomas Cox of 18 Teilo Crescent, aged 56.
- Evan John Davies of 24 Teilo Crescent, aged 42.
- Lilian Alexandra Davies of 14 Teilo Crescent, aged 37.
- John Donoghue of 21 Teilo Crescent, aged 62.
- Ronald George Evans, a visitor to Teilo Crescent, aged 19.
- James Griffiths of 31 Teilo Crescent, aged 58.
- William Frederick Griffiths of 33 Teilo Crescent, aged 16.
- Thomas George Miles of 46 Teilo Crescent, aged 37.
- Joseph Harold Stirrup, fire watcher, of 6 Teilo Crescent, aged 16.

- Matthew Walsh of 17 Creidiol Road of Teilo Crescent, aged 40.
- William Morgan Williams of 27 Teilo Crescent, aged 58.
- Alfred James Voyzey of 11 Teilo Crescent, aged 17.
- Harry Voyzey, Home Guard volunteer, of 11 Teilo Crescent, aged 19.
- Emma Catherine Williams of 27 Teilo Crescent, aged 59.
- Betty Williams of 27 Teilo Crescent, aged 20.

The firemen, Home Guard volunteers, and Civil Defence volunteers who also perished on the street:

- John Alfred Lee, firefighter, of 96 Waun Wen Road, Mayhill. Died on 20 February 1941, at Teilo Crescent, aged 36.
- Claude Stanley Kenwood, fire watcher, of 3 Eigen Crescent, Mayhill. Son of Charles Edwin Kenwood. Died on 20 February 1941, at Teilo Crescent, aged 20.
- Charles Edwin Kenwood, A.R.P. Rescue Service, of 3 Eigen Crescent, Mayhill. Father of Claude Stanley Kenwood. Died on 20 February 1941, at Teilo Crescent, aged 49.
- Reginald Herbert Daniels, fireman, A.F.S, of 24 Gomer Road, Townhill. Died on 20 February 1941, at Teilo Crescent, aged 34.
- Leonard Berry, firefighter, of 25 Nichol Street. Died on 20 February 1941, at Teilo Crescent, aged 19.
- John Collins, fire watcher, of 38 Tanymarian Road, Mayhill. Died on 20 February 1941, at Teilo Crescent, aged 16.

Swansea Records of the Blitz, 19–21 February, 1941. Teilo Crescent, Mayhill, Swansea. Walesonline.co.uk

THE BLUE HATS

Then Dulcie Jenkins got the ringworm. Everyone knew Dulcie Jenkins. She lived three doors down from us in a solid, grimy, sandstone house, two rooms down, three up, like ours. Her mother was a slommack, everyone said, her father not all there. There were numerous Jenkinses, all loud and nasal, suffering from catarrh and runny, green, gobby noses; they wore second-hand clothes nobody remembered handing down. We were not supposed to play with them, but of course we did. For one thing, Dulcie Jenkins was so bossy. She was a few years older than us, which was important then.

"You be the pages, Kezia and Drusilla," she ordered. She was in charge that day of the play we were acting on the pavement outside her house. (She made it up as she went along.)

I frowned, disoriented. I was always landed with Drusilla for a partner, just because we were twins. It wasn't fair.

"'Tis fair!" cried Dulcie. "You're the same age."

She watched to see if we knew what the word "pages" meant, what to do. Of course we did not, we were only five and starting in standard one. The two of us screwed up our faces, which had flushed red in front of the others, and Drusilla wailed, "How c'n we be pages, Dulcie?"

"Like THIS," she cried triumphantly, shooting an I-told-you-so look at the others. John Willis was the king. Dulcie, of course, was queen, and Betty Oskins was princess. "Pages is attendants, see! Ha, ha, ha, you thought they was pages in a book, di'n you?"

Dulcie bent down her ringwormed head and swept her arms to show us what to do, how to bow before a king and queen. The raw, red pinwheel "worms" on her scalp grazed our heads with our lovely golden ringlets. That was how we caught the ringworm.

At first, Mammy was beside herself. She didn't know what to do. Then she decided to take us down to Nanny's on the number 40 bus to the centre of town, where Nanny lived. Our street was up above in Townhill, which we already vaguely sensed was a poorer place, rows and rows of the grimy dark houses set in tiers overlooking town and the sea, Swansea Bay and the Mumbles in the distance. (It was curved and blue like a deep basin.) "Best view in the world, mun, from Pant Y Celyn Road!" Daddy would say, to make us glad we were living there. The streets had famous Welsh names like Dyfed, Merlin, and our own, "Powys", which somehow did not sound the same as Ashcroft, or Upper Harcourt Crescent.

The double-decker bus went down Mount Pleasant Road, swaying past the Blind Institute and the old Swansea Grammar School till it reached the bottom where stood the art gallery and Alexandra Place and, further down, Swansea Market, which was bombed.

"Mama!" (That was what Mammy called Nanny). "The kids've got ringworm!" And she began to cry in Nanny's middle room. "It's all from living in that place. I told Georgie! I told him to find us a better council house a hundred times if I told him once. We're at the bottom of the waiting list even though we've got twins!" As if we were a major misfortune – a disaster. "But he won't listen, says there's nothing left after the war, everything's bombed to bits, government got to build more. Now this happens, my precious lambs." She wept bitterly, though most of the time she shooed us outside to play on the street so she could read her novels and have a smoke. Mammy wanted a clean, new council house, no matter how small, far away from people like the Jenkinses.

Drusilla and I sat on the settee listening, and eating one of Nanny's homemade Welsh cakes from the grid-iron in the kitchen. Flour and butter, we understood, were still rationed so we were lucky to have them. We grew up with this concept without knowing it. People said things like: "Lucky ter be alive," "Lucky you got a school left," "Lucky yewer mother ran in th' bomb shelter soon as the siren gone off," "Lucky you still got 'an 'ead on yewer shoulders."

Our ringlets shone in soft, fulsome rows around our heads. The importance of hair, of its shining, golden, lustrous length and weight and the looming catastrophic loss of it, dimly emerged. I envied our older brother Davey, who seemed to have no such problem. Boys had short, clipped hair shaved by the barber back and sides.

"Well, let me see now, Mavis," said Nanny slowly, getting out the steel nit-comb from the wall-cupboard by the fireplace. "Don't get worked up." The teeth of the comb were stiff and glinting.

Obediently we proffered Nanny our heads, one by one, so she could look for nits at the same time.

"Looks bad, Mavis," said Nanny, when she was done. Nanny loved being consulted. She parted our curls and rubbed the queer, ugly red rings that were spreading over our scalps with her finger, thoughtfully. "I'd get an appointment at the clinic right away."

She gave us another Welsh cake each to take with us. They were made with margarine and powdered eggs and a couple of raisins sprinkled in the dough. "Not enough to feed a bird," she sighed, but she didn't have any coupons left for butter, and no chickens for real eggs.

The clinic was a terrible place along Alexandra Road. A dark, solid, grimy building loomed through the rain, with iron bars at some of the windows. We had to walk past the gas works and the jail to get there, and cut up by the old Swansea Market (half-standing with broken shards of glass still hanging from the ceiling after the Blitz; they were building a new one). Once inside the clinic, we were ushered into a special long room set up with temporary partitions. It was the ringworm room for the time being, said the nurse. Mammy sat on a long bench by a long, blank wall with all the other mammies. On the other wall was an old, fading wartime poster of a baby in a cot and big red words I could almost decipher: "DON'T FORGET THE ORANGE JUICE AND COD LIVER OIL." And another, more ominous: "DONT FORGET YOUR *GAS MASK*", with a horrible picture of someone that looked like a swarming prehistoric insect with a pipe coming out of its nose.

"This way, Mrs Thomas. You can undress them ready for the doctor here." A stiff woman dressed in white, with a white, winged cap perched on her head that looked like a butterfly, pointed behind a partition. Two rows of naked children, one of little boys and one of little girls, were sitting on a bench crying for their mammies.

"Dun' want to undress…"

"You got to, stop it. Undo them buttons," said the nurse sharply. She was carrying an important board with a pencil stub which she used to tick off names.

Mammy bent down and undid the buttons of our liberty-bodices that girls wore under their dresses.

"Ooh—!" Hands quickly criss-crossed our bare-naked chests. I did it first and Drusilla copied. I didn't want anyone seeing, especially my titties. We looked like two little postulants, shuffling into the examining room. Men in white with glittering stethoscopes round their necks stood by a table.

"Come along!" cried the woman doctor, dressed in a white coat. She had a stethoscope round her neck, two rubber snakes with a metal circle at the end that was magic or satanic. She pressed it to your chest and listened for something – what? At once Drusilla and I covered our titties with our hands as we walked naked down the large room to be examined fully by the tall men at the other end. The woman doctor was half amused, throwing an exasperated glance at the two male doctors who were sitting at the edge of a desk at ease, tapping their stethoscopes. They sniggered at us trying to cover our titties; the adults found it so funny, and I tried to understand why. "None of that! Take away your hands, you've got *nothing to hide*!" Mysterious words that must mean something we didn't yet know about. The woman doctor was embarrassed and getting frustrated. She jerked our hands away. At once we clamped them back, like clams, Drusilla following me again. The doctors grinned, amused, and pressed the cold metal magic circles on our chests. "Breathe in."

"Twins! Well!"

Dropped from another planet, covered with ringworm.

Where, oh where, was Mammy? Why had they taken her away from us? Why had we had to be examined alone at this great crisis in our lives, when we weren't even six?

"Are they getting their government orange juice and cod liver oil, Mrs Thomas? It's in your ration book."

The treatment was proffered. The nurse back behind the partition thrust a dark-coloured, evil-looking bottle into Mammy's hands. Iodine, she said. "Here. Use twice daily on their scalps. Shave them first. Apply for two weeks, then come back."

That evening, after tea, Mammy got out the sewing shears from her workbox. We were playing behind the curtains, trying not to be seen, peeping out through the thin netting at the other children on the street outside, from whom we were now separated as by a strange screen. They played and screamed around the lampposts in the dusk, like shadows. Where was Dulcie Jenkins?

"Who's going to be first?" said Mammy from the fireplace.

"Drusilla, she's oldest," I declared.

"Only by five minutes!" cried Drusilla. We'd heard Mammy tell Nanny that once: "They came out five minutes apart." Was that a long time ago? A secret, like so much else.

"Well, Kezia, you first."

I tried to be the bravest. Mammy cut within an inch of my scalp at first. The scissors crunched through the hair. The mat was soon littered with glossy, bright, golden curls.

Mammy was shocked, but I pranced around the living room with sudden exhilaration. So this was what it was like to be a boy, to be Davey! This freedom, this lightness! Davey stood awed by the window; what was happening to his sisters? He'd never live it down on Powys Avenue: bald sisters, two of them. Drusilla began to cry.

"How many times I washed them and turned them on my fingers…" Mammy caught up the curls in her apron and threw them in the fire. There was a sizzling and an acrid smell; the smell of singed hair.

"Mammy never kept one," we mourned sadly.

Mammy lathered one hand, and picked up Daddy's razor in the other.

"Oh… Mammy!" I did not want to be brave after all. I attempted to close my eyes.

Mammy razed a harsh furrow down my scalp. A long red weal was exposed, then more weals and rings red and pustulous. She washed the bits of hair away with special green soap, and opened the iodine bottle she'd got from the nurse. "This is going to hurt."

Our scalps roared with flame and blood, and Mammy's tears fell over the abrasions. "This is hurting me more than you."

Mammy opened the front door for a minute to let out the smell. Drusilla and I sat by the fire, suddenly chilled because of our new bald heads. I looked at Drusilla's head; it was an orange-painted ball on account of the iodine, so I knew mine must look the same because we were twins. It itched.

"Dun' scratch!" cried Mammy. "You'll get poisoned."

Daddy came home from his shift at the power station. It was late, well past our bedtime. Davey had gone upstairs to read his comics in bed, in his pyjamas, *Hotspur* and *Morgyn the Mighty*.

"Well, that's what they look like now," Mammy sniffed. We hung our heads.

"Oh ho!" roared Daddy, slinging his rucksack on the hook on the kitchen wall. He rubbed his big hands. "Look at them curls! Thought I 'ad the wrong house! Two little curly-winks!"

"No we 'aven't got curls no more, Daddy!" Drusilla screamed, breaking into a big darling smile for him.

"Yes you do," he cried. "Course you do. Curly-winks! Curly-wink a' barber."

We all ran round the table, squealing and screaming, laughing, happy again.

But later, hidden behind the curtain, I heard Mammy, passionately –

"What d'you want to laugh at it for, Cedric? How can you joke?"

"Got to pretend in front of the kids, mun. Don't do to let them see you're upset, poor buggers. Looks like it's eating their 'eads right through."

I jumped out from behind the curtain. "Oh Daddy, dun' let the worms eat my head!"

Mammy boiled our brushes and combs in dettol. Davey had to stay away from us not to catch it; ringworm was "catching", a new word. Gradually we got used to not going to school. It seemed strange to hide behind the bedroom window upstairs so our bare heads would not be seen by the kids passing up the lane by our house, hurrying before the bell. Then we heard the bell clang across the yard, shaken by a teacher, Mr Morgan, and watched the lines go in, starting with the lowest standard, the teacher standing at the head looking grim. Then quiet. You could see through the distant windows the heads of standard 1A bent over their desks, and the teacher moving up and down the rows with a cane in her hand.

After ten more days, the ringworm was cured, as the woman doctor at the clinic had predicted.

"Yes, looks like the weals is gone, Mavis," said Nanny.

"They're healed," said the doctor at the clinic, and back home everyone suddenly wept with joy for five minutes. Davey went outside with his catapult to shoot something to celebrate. The school attendance officer came and said that, strictly speaking, we should now return to school, but when he saw our bald heads with a few hairs sticking out like two chickens, he said he'd waiver it.

It was early summer now, and the last term was beginning. It was too hot to keep us inside. Mammy made us identical little hats. They were square-shaped and they fitted perfectly round each head, like an envelope. A strap went under the chin that buttoned firmly at the side over our ears, so kids couldn't pull them off. The hats were blue. Mammy embroidered a row of white daisies around the border. We were to wear the hats all the time in school, even at recess outside, playing in the yard, until our hair grew back. Special permission had been granted, of course, by Miss Prouse, the headmistress.

The hats created a sensation that Monday morning. Everyone swarmed around the Thomas twins, everyone wanted to be our special friend and stand next to us in line. But nobody actually mentioned the hats. By some unspoken code this was regarded as unforgiveably mean. Even though, in the ensuing weeks, all eyes were glued to the Thomas twins' hats and the row of daisies under which pushed a few recalcitrant hairs. Nobody ever uttered the question that hovered like a cypher over the yard and school precincts: *What is it like under the Thomas twins' hats?*

Then suddenly, everyone seemed to forget. Nice weather had come. Daisies popped up in the inside courtyard, and Miss Milne let standard one sit out there and make daisy chains; we sat at the edge of the grass in the sunshine that showered down through the glass roof, our small fingers struggling to pinch holes in the stems. "Like this, Kezia. *He loves me, he loves me not…*" hummed Miss Milne, counting her chain. At playtime we skipped furiously with the others, we hopped around the hopscotch squares, we played two-balls madly against the lavatory walls as if our lives depended on it. "Onesies, twosies, buckle yewer shoesies…' Only the teachers remembered the blue hats and were Specially Nice to the Thomas twins.

But then, we were moving away, leaving Powys Avenue at last and the hill of houses overlooking town! Our name had finally come up on the housing list, beamed Daddy. We were getting a brand-new council house on a council estate by the sea in a place called the Mumbles, all thanks to somebody called Clement Atlee and 'is Labour gov'ment, stressed Daddy. He had hired a lorry, and his weight-lifting pals were going to help with the move. One of them was a tough little man called Teify, who was the Welsh welterweight champion, said Daddy proudly. Teify was going to carry the settee out to the kerb all by himself, on his back.

It was real. The new house near the Mumbles was by the sea, and had an upstairs *and* a downstairs lavatory, boasted Drusilla at playtime. (We were famous again in school, the Thomas twins and their brother Davey, escaping the Jenkinses to something better.) "And it's spotless clean an' hygenic," Drusilla added significantly, repeating Mammy's words, though neither of us had a clue what "hygenic" meant.

On the last day of term we were summoned to Miss Prouse's office. There was a chair outside the headmistress's door, where monitors dropped off the registers in the morning after attendance was called. Neither of us had ever been given this honour; Miss Milne had always singled out Gwynneth Rhys or Percy Rideout. But that day Miss Milne had chosen me, perhaps because she was sorry about my bald head under the blue hat. I carried the long pink register to the private room at the end of the corridor, where all was hushed. I'd dropped it and run. Now Drusilla, the forward one, knocked on that door.

"Wonder what it's for." Drusilla wriggled with anticipation. We wondered if it might not be a little goodbye present from the headmistress since we were leaving... we had attended the school from infants up.

Drusilla knocked again, and a voice went, "Come in." We entered timidly. Miss Prouse was sitting behind a great oak desk, with a glass inkpot and the class registers on it, a big, solid woman with a sloping bust. The room was almost in darkness, each wall lined with heavy volumes. There was a painting on the wall behind her of a shipwreck in Swansea Bay, with turbulent seas. The one window was closely shuttered. There was a queer-patterned carpet on the parquet floor, and our eyes fixed on this.

"So... you're leaving us, Kezia and Drusilla," Miss Prouse purred. As she spoke, perfume wafted out of her mouth and we sensed the rustle of silk and the jingling of her bracelet. "Just when you were getting on so well."

She was rising from the dreaded chair and moving inexplicably towards us and past us to the door behind. We heard the low click of the lock. Then she returned to the chair, which also was heavy, with arms.

"As it's your last day," Miss Prouse said softly, "and you won't be coming back again, I was wondering…" She hesitated. "I have a favour to ask." She paused. "Would you remove your hats for me to see… just this once?"

Obediently, each of us loosened the chin strap buttoned on the side that Mammy had warned us never to undo, never let anyone see. We slipped off the blue hats, feeling naked. Our shiny bald heads with new speckles of hairs glowed in the darkness. There was a queer silence. When we looked up, Miss Prouse's eyes were glittering.

"You can put them back on now," she whispered. "And – *here*." She fumbled in her purse and pulled out two big brown pennies and pressed one in each of our hands. You could buy a liquorice with a penny.

"Oh! *Thank* you, Miz Prouse!" we chorused.

Miss Prouse gave a little cough. "Of course, we needn't… er… mention this to anyone, need we? Our little secret…"

We shook our heads; it was my first experience of the adult world, and of evil.

THE BEST GAME OF ALL

Every May, the hawthorns at the edge of the woods behind our house burst into bloom. You wondered how the trees knew, frothing white blossoms heavy with perfume floating up. You'd forgotten the rush of whiteness, the radiance. It was where we now lived, on a housing estate near the Mumbles, overlooking Swansea Bay and the Mumbles pier.

Hidden thorns and prickles caught at you, as we well knew, tearing your skin as you burrowed under to hide, but the blossoms were so light we didn't mind, so sweet-smelling. The aroma carried as far as the pipe-iron bridge by the stream, as far even as the respectable line of private houses on Grange Road where people like Dr Gwyn lived.

You had to crawl under the bushes on your hands and knees. Inside it was dark, even mid-afternoon, deep under the foliage, hidden from the adults – what better place. We girls edged along over dirt and leaf mould like animals, despite our fresh frocks, to reach the den, but that only made it more secret and also dangerous, the danger of being trapped in there with no exit behind you if boys came along.

There was just enough space for Trisha to place the toy teapot and dinky cups and spoons on the wood plank that served as a table, and for the four of us girls to scrunch down, waiting for her to pour nicely and begin.

"What would you like in your tea, Mrs T, one or two?'

Of course, at eleven years old we were really too old for dolls and tea sets, but it was still one of the best games to play before it was too late… too late for what? Pretending to be grown-ups, mothers, of course, before we were actually able to become so, which might happen soon, very soon, hinted Trish. She was the eldest by six months, nearly twelve, and she had long, flaxen hair loose to her waist, like a princess. She knew Everything from her older sister, Marge. "Periods" were soon going to happen to each of us, because we were girls. Blood would come out between your legs, which meant you could then have a baby if you went with a boy. No one knew what this word "went" exactly involved, but Trish claimed knowledge.

"What happens to the blood, then, Trish?" We didn't really believe this.

"You wears things, cloths, between yewer legs to catch it, my sister showed me. More tea, Mrs Bevan?"

Beryl nodded.

So we returned to the serious business of being Mrs Thomas, Mrs Matthews, Mrs Morgan and Mrs Bevan, our celluloid dolls propped on our knees, the spiky May branches pushing into our backs like pricks. We sipped pretend tea from the cups and saucers from Trish's sister's old tea set. There was a small tin kettle we'd salvaged from the tips. Beryl had sneaked a lace doily from her mother's sideboard.

"Was that one lump or two, Mrs T?"

"Oh just one, thank you, Mrs M," I said. "Got to watch my goitre.'

I pretended to smoke like my mother, waving a twig as I sipped.

"My Popsy is poorly today, an' I got a touch of arthritic myself." Popsy was Beryl's doll. It had a flat face like Mrs Bevan's, and rosebud lips she'd kiss. My own doll was pink and white and was called Elizabeth Victoria after Princess Elizabeth. King George VI, her father, was stricken at home in Buckingham Palace, expected to die any moment and then the princess would become queen. Drusilla's doll was Margaret Rose, named after Princess Margaret,

Princess Elizabeth's sister, because Drusilla and I were twins, and so had to be the same, which we secretly disliked. Our dolls were identical: pink celluloid faces with celluloid curls clustered round their dear waxen cheeks we washed and kissed; big, unblinking eyes.

Trisha's doll Heidi could blink. The brush lashes of her eyes moved up and down, and when you tipped the doll forward it went "Ma–ma!" from somewhere in its stomach. Thrilling. Do it again, Trish. Then we each got a turn making Heidi say Mama, the best word in the world, that could made you tighten and cry.

"I think she needs her feed now," hinted Trish shyly.

Silently we smiled at each other, our secret, and lifted our woollies up without a sound, exposing our tits. We pressed our dolls' hard celluloid lips to our nipples to suckle. My arms cradled Elizabeth protectively; I felt the power of my love gush out of my flat chest, my two hard, red nipples that Trisha said would one day swell into big tits for a real baby to suck.

"Ooh it's lovely, aye," sighed Trish, a warm fuzzy feeling.

Beryl was rocking hers with a swimmy look in her eyes, back and forth. She had her heels curled under her; everyone content, suckling their babies like real mothers.

"I c'n hear boys."

Trisha stopped suckling. Everything stopped. Sure enough, you could hear boys beating their way through the undergrowth down by the pipe-iron bridge – whack! Boys were violent, destructive beings. It was because of the war, said Nanny. Smash! would go the little blue robin eggs in the nest, and the mother robin would beat the air frantically with frenzied wings over the broken shells on the ground. The boys were coming closer, how close? I clutched Elizabeth Victoria.

Drusilla sniggered, so did Trish.

"Shush, they're gonna hear us." We put our arms instinctively round our dolls, which suddenly looked foolish and babyish in the underground den.

"There's girls in there, under the 'awthorns somewhere, I c'n smell 'em."

Dicky Harris, catapult in hand, suddenly pushed through the undergrowth on his knees, blinking; he was only eight. He beamed under a thick brown thatch of hair. Trevor Jones and Jeffrey Morris followed on all fours; Trevor was six and Jeffrey Morris seven. Just little boys, nevertheless with a virulent sort of animal energy and power that all boys had.

"Whew! Look at what they got here."

So this was what girls did on their own in the woods on a sunny afternoon. The boys were amused. We frowned. Boys spoiled it. Quickly we pulled our woollies down, the magic broken.

"Hey, lookat, a kettle, mun," sniggered Trevor. He gave it a kick. He had a round baby face with freckles; well, he was the youngest.

"Stoppit!" said Drusilla. "That's OURS."

Trisha twirled her long hair, and was suddenly coy.

Trevor pulled a face. Even he understood *ours* and *theirs*, *mine* and *yewers*. Besides, being younger, we could push him out and he'd miss the fun. So he crouched down under the heavy boughs with Dicky and Jeffrey, squeezing in companionably, as if he were expecting something. There was a moment's silence.

"You wanna see something?" sniggered Dicky. He had blazing blue eyes; it was as if you were waiting for something, something to happen you wanted to know about, and now it was.

I pulled up my skirt.

"Oooh, you'll get it if Mammy finds out," whispered Drusilla. I was the daring one in some things.

"She's not gonna find out."

Dicky Harris unbuttoned his short serge trousers that came to the knees, which boys wore even in winter. He was short and stocky and nice. I dropped my knickers and everyone giggled. "Ooh, I'm not looking," said Trish, but of course she did.

The boys' faces puckered anxiously as they took in what was between my legs.

"She got nothin'," they echoed in horror.

"Girls dun have nuthin'," sighed Dicky.

Disappointment, sniggers, fear, a tremor of fearful wonder why girls didn't have anything, and why was that? Dicky held on to himself anxiously.

And there it was again, that faint horrified thrill of seeing yourself as a boy saw you; boys just couldn't get over it, the nothingness of girls when they knew *something* was there. That was the secret.

"So where's 'er jinny, then?" They peered in awe. I didn't know, neither did Trish. Something hidden, you didn't find out till you were married. Trisha sniggered, she couldn't wait.

Dicky's thing was wobbling, small and pink like a little sausage, with pretty things hanging underneath. I'd never seen my brother's because our mother always pushed the bedroom door shut. "Go away, big eyes."

"You're a bad girl!" cried Dicky.

"No I'm not! You're only eight, so it doesn't count."

And then I got on top of him, lying over him, and it was if you'd always known. You knew it was what you'd been waiting for all along in the den, panting fast. Dicky was choking, he said he couldn' breathe. "Get off, Kezia mun."

Afterwards, the boys were bored. They were tired of the long hot afternoon, they said, they wanted to go 'ome for their tea. They scrambled out suddenly, tearing their trousers. The sun glowed low over the frothing white blossoms, the air sickly sweet.

The day fell flat. We could hear them bashing their way back up through the bushes with their wooden swords. Then they were gone, wheeling away on their imaginary steeds; "Whoa, away!" into the dusk.

The last of the twilight fell over the sea. We left the hawthorns and came up the embankment to the back of the estate. Slowly the lights at the backs of the houses came on, one by one. As we watched from the field we could see our mothers and fathers, outlined and lit up in the kitchen windows; they were doing things like lighting the gas, peeling potatoes at the sink for dinner, moving about in familiar motions, ordinary, commonplace, yet so full of mystery and significance. We were certain – yes, quite certain – that the best game of all was yet to come.

MORGAN LE FAY

"Good Lord, Emmie, look at them knees," cried Aunty Blod, whose full name was Blodwyn. I had just come in from playing down the woods. "Football knees!"

She was sitting on the settee in the front room having a cup of tea with Nanny. She and Nanny were visiting for the afternoon and they wore felt hats. They shook their heads, Aunty Blod comically, and Nanny more alarmed. What was I doing going down the woods by myself, a girl of just nine? I should be in the house with my twin sister Drusilla, who stood there with a plate of scones Mammy had just baked, pulling a face at me as if I was doolally.

I didn't let on. I'd been climbing the highest tree, as high as I could, as high as Hugh Griffiths' climb. I wanted to be valorous, like the Knights of the Round Table Miss Woolley was now reading to us in standard three. I did not tell them about the Quest for the Holy Grail that Miss Woolley had recently set before us. It was too intimate and tender. She had finished reading us the story of Christian in *Pilgrim's Progress*, Christian's journey from the City of Destruction to the Celestial City carrying his burden of sins on his back. Hugh Griffiths had played Christian in the little weekly plays Miss Woolley let us act in front of the class. He'd knelt before a cross drawn on the blackboard and his burden of sins – Miss Woolley's handbag strapped to his back – had plopped to the floor. Miss Woolley's lipstick and powder compact and her TCP drops had rolled across the boards. There'd been a gasp of horror but also secret delight.

"Patricia, pick up the lipstick and powder and such," Miss Woolley had said calmly. Oh we had fun and wonderful times!

There'd been a sigh of disappointment when Christian finally reached the Celestial City and *Pilgrim's Progress* came to an end. But Miss Woolley soon revived us. She brought out another book, *King Arthur and His Knights*. Now we had a new vocabulary: chivalry, valour, honour, tournament, jousting, courtesy and mercy. The highest deed one could perform was to show mercy, said Miss Woolley. You'd be on the point of slicing off someone's ears or your enemy's head, and at the last minute, you didn't; you showed mercy. "To err is human; to forgive divine," she quoted, switching venues in literature as she often did. Oh it was grand, in her class.

I rubbed the dirt off my knees with my hands and then rubbed them clean on the back of my dress. No one ever washed their hands, unless they were filthy from working in the garden or helping Daddy pick up cow manure in the fields for the roses.

"You should be out the kitchen helping your mother, like Drusilla," frowned Nanny.

Drusilla smirked. She was wearing exactly the same dress as me, identical red tartan cotton with a big tartan bow in her hair, since we were twins. I could never escape it, no matter how many oak trees I climbed.

"Not like 'er twin, is she, Emmie?" said Aunty Blod of me.

Miss Woolley had said "Right always conquers". The sun had filtered through the long Doric windows of the classroom, as in church, as Miss Woolley assured us, in her low, soothing voice, that the knight must rescue his own soul by overcoming giants and demons. Only then could he aspire to a vision of the Mysteries and the Holy Grail. Of course we hadn't a clue what such words meant, but were thrilled nevertheless, we boys and girls, as we sat stock-still at our wooden desks, hands in laps. Miss Woolley expected us to *imagine* what such words meant, that of course she knew were way too advanced for us. Miss Woolley believed in speaking to children with imagination and power – perhaps she had the second sight; I'd heard someone say that once of her.

Miss Woolley had also started telling us about *The Black Book of Carmarthen*, written in Welsh, which she kept in her high desk, with the lid down, which she would read to us one day *when we were ready*.

Black Book? Welsh?

Auntie Blod affected horror and Nanny put down her Worcester china cup, truly concerned. In her opinion it sounded satanic. Drusilla pulled another mocking face; she'd never heard of *The Black Book of Carmarthen*, she didn't *want* to, she scorned. She was in a different class from me where she learned how to roll and flute pastry – "Far more useful," Nanny opined.

"Miss Woolley is batty." Drusilla tapped her head, twirling her finger against her temple, meaning not all there, like me.

"Well. We never 'eard words like them in our schooldays," said Aunty Blod, who was short and fat with a round, merry, red face. She was Nanny's sister and not at all like her. I understood she was of a lower class to Nanny, and therefore to us, but she was awfully merry and chuckled warmly at us. She told "bad" – meaning dirty – jokes about bananas that drove Daddy mad. He told Mammy we mustn't listen to them, it would affect our minds. He didn't say this directly to us; he didn't want to acknowledge such things, that was Mammy's job. "Yewer Aunt Blodwyn 'as a dirty mouth," he'd say to Mammy, and Mammy would laugh and say, "Oh Auntie Blod is the salt of the earth."

"What the 'ell does she mean, the 'Oly Grail?" said Auntie Blod, affecting shock. She once said at the wake after a funeral that the Baptist minister was "warming 'is backside in front of the fire". Daddy was furious and had stomped out, refusing to be in the same room as "that woman".

I felt Aunty Blod and Nanny weren't taking Holy Grails and Mysteries seriously enough. Miss Woolley had said that the druids had their own Golden Key to the Mysteries. Right away, I was sorry. I thought of Miss Woolley and her shining round face and frizzy curls and her high sense of honour. Somehow I'd let her down, exposing her to Auntie Blod's and Nanny's amusement. I felt remorse, a sharp stab in my belly.

"Maybe this Miss Woolley is a spiritualist," they joked.

Miss Woolley loved us; she told us stories that lasted for months.

Mammy brought in a tray with fresh tea.

"Yewer Kezia ain't 'alf a one," said Aunty Blod. "Swallered 'alf the dictionary."

I'd said again, shyly, for I felt I should try to be brave and salve Miss Woolley's honour in the new spirit of the Holy Grail, that Miss Woolley believed in great literature for children. She hoped we'd read the Black Book for ourselves one day, translated into English, when we were older, in a higher standard. *The Black Book of Carmarthen* went back to maybe before the Dark Ages.

"Well I don't like the sound of *that*," said Nanny.

***

There were rules. There was order. Punishments. Every morning, first thing before the register, the teacher knew when, we had to stand to attention and line out in order, row by row, into the big centre hall of the school. A saintly old hall with the scent of All Saints Church. Long stained-glass windows with long cords hanging down. You lined in, in silence; you were not to look each side of you but straight ahead – you'd get a smack across the ear for looking around. I didn't have the words then for it, but you felt the teachers' power; it was about power, and they had it and you did not, and that was right, of course.

The morning light fell dimly through the windows high up in slants. A teacher up the front we couldn't see played an opening chord on the school piano.

"There is a green hill far away
Without a city wall,
Where our dear Lord was crucified..."

A mysterious hymn, a sad one, but we sang in our heavy, lilting child voices, frightened of something, something about the big hall and the teachers standing sternly in a row down the sides. Then there was a prayer read by Mr Rowland, the head teacher, who was bent over in a hoop at the rostrum like Nanny, followed by a passage from the Bible. We sat on the floor looking up at him, waiting. A psalm today. "I will lift up mine eyes unto the 'ills," he went in a squeaky old voice. There were strange words in the psalm. "He shall not suffer thy foot to be moved." Full of mystery because we did not know what that could possibly mean, but it must be something holy: God not suffering, not letting our feet be moved around? It must be something secret, it was so strange.

"The Lord is thy shade on thy right hand?" quivered Mr Rowland. He peered over the rim of his glasses at us, including the teachers. That was frightening, too. What was it about the right? What happened to the left; why was there no shade for the left hand?

And last of all, the most frightening of all: "The Lord shall preserve thy going out and thy coming in from this time forth, even forever more." You knew this meant more than going in and out of a door – but what? "Inside you," said Miss Woolley.

The way the teachers stood like sentinels on either side of the hall, not moving, not blinking, on guard.

***

Miss Woolley didn't hit us, she didn't smack our faces like Miss Bailiss did in standard one when I was six, and Miss Davis in standard two. Miss Bailiss made you put out your hand, and you shook, and *whack* with the cane across your palm and made it burn. Drusilla had cried and I was too frightened to say, "No! No! Pleased dun' hurt my sister." Last year, in standard two, Miss Davis called me out the front for talking. "Come out here – *you*, Kezia Thomas." Balled fists lambasted my ears, in front of the class, everybody watching - *bam!* Her two fists at the same time on each side of my ears. My brains burst, my head was wobbling awful. Miss Davis smirked. "Now get back to your seat, Kezia Thomas. That'll teach you to shrug your shoulders at *me* when spoken to!" *You cheeky kid from the council houses.*

I didn't cry. Something awful was happening in my head, and my writing wouldn't slope the same on the lines after that, but lucky Mammy and Daddy never noticed.

***

Benedicta Morgan had green eyes and two long black plaits, which I envied. When the school nurse came to inspect our heads, calling out each child's name in turn by alphabetical order, the girls with plaits were ordered to undo them. When Benedicta loosened hers, her hair fell in a thick black cape flowing to her waist, and my envy knew no bounds.

Now Benedicta Morgan was coming up behind me on the path after school. She had her mackintosh slung over her shoulder like a knight's cloak, and a penknife stuck in her belt.

The woods closed in one side right up to the path, and a tall wire fence closed in on the other. A lonely path, with barely room to pass, which was why my father always warned me, in a gruff voice, against taking this way home. "You take the main road like yewer sister." You heard of vague men lurking in the bushes, waiting for little girls like me to come along. Which was surely all part of the test, and the mystery, a certain dread, the way the little dirt path wended through tall flowers and grasses, a bird singing suddenly; it was lovely, too.

As Benedicta caught up with me, her leather shoes thudding, my hands tightened at the ready in case she was planning to bash my head in again. She'd already done it once at the bottom of Linden Hill where I lived, down by the oak tree. (The Morgans lived on Sycamore Road at the top of our hill. Benedicta had an older brother of eighteen and a younger sister; her father was at sea, which sounded romantic.) It had been an unfair attack, taking me off-guard, deliberately, without warning. "First one down wins," her friend Phyllis, who was nearly twelve, had challenged. She was much older than me, I was only nine, and she lived next door to the Morgans on Sycamore. She'd decided the rules right off, before I could have any say or think this was a fight. Benedicta swung me off-balance to the ground by my mackintosh belt and jumped on top of me, straddling my belly. She banged my head hard into the ground by my hair and pinned my arms back, but I didn't cry out. Her eyes were blazing above mine; I caught sight of tiny glittering white teeth. "Morgan" was a powerful Welsh name, and her name, Benedicta, also had a sort of church sound more potent than my old English one, Kezia.

But I'd fought back, scrabbling at her face with my nails and pushing up my legs. Suddenly, I was the one on top. "GIRLS' FIGHT!" everyone yelled, and Irene Jenkins and Gwynneth Jones and her little brothers and other kids appeared from nowhere, gathering round excitedly in a ring. "Bash 'er 'ead in!" "Give it to 'er!"

Phyllis Jones pulled me off when she saw I was the one on top and winning. "Benedicta won," she lied.

"No she didn't!"

The kids drew back. They all knew she hadn't won.

It was inconclusive. My knees were bleeding proudly. Benedicta had scrambled to her feet, shaken, her head full of leaves and her mac torn. Now she'd get it from Mrs Morgan, her mother.

Now Benedicta had caught up to me on the path. She was smiling nicely and I knew why. She wanted me to put her down to be Morgan le Fay in the class play "The Holy Grail". I'd been holding off my decision. Beautiful Benedicta with her shining black hair that fell to the waist. Mammy kept my brown hair shorter and sensible below the ears so I wouldn't get lice. Who else but Benedicta could be Morgan le Fay? Le Fay was the most beautiful of King Arthur's nine sisters. She lived with her maidens on the winterless Isle of Avalon, enchantress and healer, keeper of the Holy Grail, intoned Miss Wooley. But she could also turn suddenly into something else, evil and powerful, which was why everyone wanted to be her in the play, for her heathen power. She had cast a spell over Arthur to make her brother love her even though they were brother and sister and she had borne his son, a circumstance Miss Woolly passed over quickly.

"I'm a Morgan," Benedicta had flashed after class. That was true. Morgan was a powerful Welsh name, everyone knew that, more powerful than my own, Thomas. But I was the one Miss Wooley had assigned the job of casting; I was in charge.

Miss Woolly had nodded to me across the rows. "Kezia will choose the cast." Dear old Miss Woolly of standard three, with her frizzy, peppery-red hair in tight curls round her face! She had glowing eyes in which she put TCP drops every morning to protect them from germs.

Everyone had heard her words and turned to look, including Benedicta. I'd had nine out of ten on my composition. (You never were given ten out of ten, not to make you conceited and full of yourself.) The sentence Miss Woolly had particularly liked, reading it aloud to the class, was: "I ran down the back path with all the joy of spring past Mammy hanging out the washing on the line, Daddy's underpants and vests and Mammy's nightie and sheets from the bed billowing in the wind, and next door in the back garden Mrs Jinks' big bloomers blowin' in the wind."

"WH-A-T?" Mammy had screamed that evening, going red in the face and snatching up the exercise book. She read as fast as she could. "You wrote *that!*" My mother was screaming, laughing, what a lark!

You felt safe with Miss Woolly, loved, without her really saying so. She sat at the high teacher's desk by the coal fire in her pressed silk blouse and long serge skirt, peering out over her spectacles. Each morning she read to us about the sacred Order of the Garter, chivalry towards the weak, about King Arthur and his Knights of the Round Table. Her voice would purr in a mellifluous way.

***

Benedicta was looking at me intently. "Have you made your mind up yet, Kezia?" she said softly, seductively, being specially nice. I could feel her yearning, wanting it, desiring to have the role of Morgan le Fay in the play on Thursday.

I hesitated, relishing the moment, my power to deny Benedicta and keep the part of Morgan le Fay for myself. (Elizabeth Hadley was to have the only other important part for girls, the mysterious Lady of the Lake that Miss Woolley had specially reserved for her.) I did not ask why she got special treatment; I already knew. It was Elizabeth's cool speaking voice and pretty dresses and nice manners, and most of all, that she was a Mumbles girl, born and bred in the Mumbles; her family had been here for generations. Benedicta and I were just come from a council house estate that Elizabeth Hadley's family would remember as originally being the old farm, old Vernons' place. And now we town usurpers were here from goodness knew where, from the poor of Hafod or Cwmbwrla or Townhill (another housing estate where the Thomas twins *had actually caught ringworm*). The inhabitants of our estate were culled from everywhere by the Labour government after the war. What to do with us all, the poor left over from the war? Build us housing on beautiful farmland by the sea, houses with two lavatories and a fireplace, and front and back gardens, all subsidised by the taxes of the people of the Mumbles. I'd heard such things said in back lanes and in shops as people waited in line for pastries and bread and Welsh cakes. "Some of them are smart."

"Aw right, Benedicta," I relented. "You can be Morgan le Fay."

"Good kid." She linked arms, as friends.

Ever since the fight, I'd been practising in the back garden with Father's dumbbells from his weight-lifting to build up the muscles in my arms. I felt the surge in each bicep as I struggled to lift each iron ball, my hands trembling with the exertion, my eyes bulging. "What the 'ell's that Kezia Thomas doing down the garden with them dumbbells?" I'd heard Benny Jinks say, Mrs Jinks' grown-up son, peering through their kitchen window. I wanted to be able to bash Benedicta Morgan's head in one day. I was sure I was now ready should the moment present itself.

Benedicta was smiling, the full sensuous smile of Morgan le Fay, enchantress. She shifted her cloak over her shoulder now she was sure of herself, her penknife glinting; she'd got what she wanted.

"Hey." She nudged me. "There's a boy coming down the path."

A small boy of about six, standard one, was coming towards us head down, humming to himself. "Let's get 'im!" said Benedicta.

She stepped forward and blocked his path. The little boy looked up, startled.

"And just where d'you think you're going all alone, my boy?" said Benedicta in a new, deep, authoritative voice. She gave him a push.

At once he began to whimper, "Please dun' hurt me, I'm jus' goin' 'ome."

"And who said you can use this path? Answer me!"

The little boy blinked, his hands clamped between his trouser legs. He had on the short grey serge trousers to the knees little boys wore, with a row of buttons down the crotch boys had to unbutton to pee, and grimy wool knee socks.

"Please, please dun' hurt me, oh please, please let me off this time."

Benedicta smiled slowly and gave me a wink. "Well, you have to give us a look, first. Go on, undo your buttons an' pull out your willy or I'll cut it off."

She touched her penknife.

Tears spilled down his cheek. I felt the rush of power. Yes, we'd see it sticking out wobbling and pink and he'd have to stand there like that till we said.

"Please, please, no." The little boy's eyes were shut tight. Pee began to trickle down his trouser leg onto his sock, and I felt sorry then, frightened.

"Aw let him go, Benedicta, he's only little," I said, as an excuse.

The boy shot me a look of such hope.

Benedicta hesitated, disappointed, but she wanted to be Morgan le Fay.

"We-ell, we'll let you off this time. But this is my path and I don't want to catch you coming this way again! And don't you tell nobody, see!"

The boy shot off, his plump legs disappearing through waves of dust. He was gone. The moment hung long and hot and dizzying.

Something had changed, everything, the heat arising from the woods, the bright distant sky, the sudden strange call of a bird.

I followed Benedicta up the path, knowing I would never fight again, that there was a hidden power I'd not suspected in one small boy whose wounding was my own, and that therein lay a Mystery.

'ER ROYAL 'IGHNESS

Skeggs was the new girl. She sat up the front in standard four, her large eyes fluttering, her sandy-red hair hanging limp. When Miss Gruffith called upon her to read aloud to see what she could do, there was silence afterwards, for the new girl enunciated beautifully. "Olga Skeggs articulates every word distinctly," said Miss Gruffith approvingly. Skeggs said *your* like Princess Elizabeth, not like our local Welsh *yewer*, and she'd say *hello* in a cool, clear tone instead of our *hi-ya*, which was not strictly a word at all. She never dropped her aitches. "My father says there's no such thing as *h*eaven," she said, the *h* accentuated. We were momentarily awed.

Out in the yard at recess, the new girl refused to answer to "Olga". "Just call me Skeggs!" she cried, tossing her skimpy pigtails, her eyes fluttering, her mouth twitching. And straight away you knew where she'd got that from – wanting to be called by her surname like a boy. She was copying George in the Enid Blyton "Fives" books we'd all read – *Five Have Plenty of Fun, Five Get Into Trouble* – tales of confident, well-fed English children having romping good times away from boarding school and speaking to each other in a fascinating elite lingo – "Jolly good sport", "I say, let's be chums!" – far removed from our Welsh working-class lives, George the most so, the most daring girl ever. For one thing she had a big dog of her own that she insisted accompany her everywhere; her hair was cut in short boyish curls like our brothers'. She refused to answer to "Georgina" but insisted on being called "George" –

"Call me George!" – a boy's name, not a sissy girl's she'd scorn. We'd never met anyone like her in our library books.

Olga tossed her head. "Call me Skeggs!" she insisted.

The new girl did not bow her head and close her eyes for the Lord's Prayer in the morning, "on principle," she said in a queer tight voice. Her father, Mr Skeggs, said that religion was the opium of the people, she challenged, screwing up her face in a funny way. He was an *atheist*, she added proudly, which sounded a terrible thing to be but which somehow made Skeggs special, as if she and Mr Skeggs could see something about us we couldn't. To our amazement, Miss Gruffith said it was all right, Olga Skeggs was not required to bow her head and pray to God.

"I was born in Eng-er-land, in the Worral," said Skeggs one day outside at recess.

"Where zat?"

"Chester."

We marvelled again. A girl not born in Wales, not from our seaside village of the Mumbles, surrounded by hills and eternal low cloud. I felt a stab of envy.

"But yewer father's Welsh, all the same, isn't he?" I challenged. Mr Skeggs was originally from Merthyr, a coal mining area. "Besides, the Worral's not in England, it belongs to us." I had a vague idea of the Welsh Marches.

"It doesn't!" flashed Skeggs, her face turning as orange as her hair, two bright spots on each cheek. "The Domesday Book cites it as on the *east s*ide of the River Dee, near Chester, England."

That settled that, for the moment; for one thing about Skeggs, she seemed to know her history which, of course, she did not pronounce as *'istry*.

"Huh, just showing off, wanting attention, trying to make out she's special when she isn't. All that flutt'ring her eyes! Who does she think she is, 'er royal 'ighness?" scoffed my sister Drusilla. "Her father's just a fishmonger!"

No one, of course, would ever say such a thing to Skeggs. Everyone was extra nice to the new girl, for how awful for your father to be "on the fish". You saw Mr Skeggs in Swansea Market on a Saturday, lugging bales of hake and bass on his back fresh off the boats and throwing them on the slab at the fishmonger's. "Mornin'! Nice piece o"ake, nice rounds o' cod!" he'd holler, as you shopped with your mother. "Pint o' cockles fresh from the sands!" That was Penclawdd, where the cockle women stood in the water at low tide filling their baskets. Mr Skeggs' hands were raw and red with cold from handling ice, chopping the heads and tails off the fish, pulling out the entrails and tossing them in the slop bucket behind the counter. He had on a wool cap and a long linen apron smeared with blood. You pretended not to notice, looking the other way as he wrapped Mother's hake in a sheet of brown paper, and of course, not let on to Skeggs at school; that would have been regarded as terribly mean.

So Skeggs joined us in all our games, hop-scotch and three balls and skipping. She gamely climbed the highest tree, jumped the concrete blocks on the sea-shore, crawled into the concrete bunker left on the beach from the war even though she was afraid of spiders. Of course, being an atheist meant she was left out of all the fun of Band of Hope at Bethany Baptist chapel on a Thursday night, in the Mumbles. Trish and Gwynneth and Drusilla and I attended though we weren't strictly nonconformist. Reverend Pritchard, who by day was the local post-man, presented a lantern slide show of "Dr Livingstone in Africa", after prayers and a hymn, "Blest are the pure in heart". We sat in rows on hard benches in the dimmed light in the little social hall, gazing up at the screen while we chewed toffees and liquorice. After the lantern show, we took part in performances on the dais: you could get up and sing or recite a poem, and Archie Evans in standard two would stand up and imitate bird songs, trilling and whistling – throttling his larynx beautiful, cried Mrs Pritchard.

Olwen Pritchard was stout with tight permed ringlets around her face. She wore a stiff, dark dress with a lace collar and solid, clumpy shoes befitting a Baptist's wife; she gave us cake and biscuits, and pop to drink afterwards, and we said "Thank yew, Missis Pritchard."

Then the reverend closed with the Dismissal, raising his hands and eyes towards the ceiling, "The grace of our Lord Jesus Christ, and the love of God, and the fellowship of the 'Oly Spirit, be with us all evermore, amen." We did not yet doubt that this was absolutely true. Oh it was grand! I could only wish that Skeggs were there. But Skeggs came with us only as far as the top of the lane and then hung back, her eyes brimming with tears for she cried easily, often hugging her arms to her chest. She would not cross the door of a chapel, true to her father's principles, which were something called *proletarian*.

The sea shone like diamonds, the trees frilled with crisp, burning leaves, and the air breezed fresh and salty as we ran along the shore that September with our swimsuits. One last bathe! We ran into the waves that were lilting and fresh, screaming with joy, Trish and Drusilla and Beryl Evans and Gwynneth, all of us. Skeggs stood whimpering at the edge of the water, huddled in her clothes. She wasn't allowed in because of her "ee-ers", she said. "I've got drops in my ee-ers," she called. She had cotton-wool balls stuffed in them to protect them; Mr Skeggs had warned they mustn't get wet.

"Wasser marrer with 'er?" called Trish over the waves. "What's she crying about now?"

"She can't come in because of 'er yers, she'll get heck from 'er father."

***

Mr Skeggs was a card-carrying communist. He believed in world revolution – which it seemed was just a matter of time away – when the workers of the world would unite to smash the capitalist state, overthrow the monarchy, abolish private ownership and, in particular, take over all the newspapers. If our landless parents in their council houses did but realise, they were part of the forces of history that someone called Marx – revered by Mr Skeggs – had said were moving inexorably towards a higher evolution of communism. For Mr Skeggs studied dialectical materialism in between his fish rounds.

"Bloody nutcase, known all over the estate," said Daddy genially to Mother. So that sounded all right then, even exciting, to visit Skeggs and be the friend of a Red.

"Your father works in the power station, don't he?"

Mr Skeggs eyed me carefully as I sat on the couch in the living room. He was a small, thin man with black hair greased straight back, and a black, clipped moustache like Joseph Stalin. He'd come in from the market reeking of fish, changed his clothes immediately out in the kitchen, and had a cup of tea brought him by Mrs Skeggs, an excitable, quivering woman in a worn blouse and long, thin skirt. She had the same orange hair as Skeggs.

"Yes, Mr Skeggs, he's on the turbines, sir," I added.

I'd already surmised from the library books on the shelf, *The Communist Manifesto, War and Peace, Hard Times* – Mr Skeggs' regular reading fare – that my father's job, which involved heavy labour, opening and shutting valves on the turbine floor of the power station, would be cause for respect.

"Good union man," nodded Mr Skeggs approvingly, and Skeggs glowed. It seemed I'd passed the test. I blinked. I only knew that my father often shook his head at his weekly payslip, saying "Nuthin' much left, mun, after union dues."

The fire crackled in the grate. The Skeggses lived in a tiny prefab, one of rows and rows of prefabricated bungalows on the lower hill of the council house estate, put up by Clement Attlee's Labour government after the war. We lived in the tin houses higher up the hill. They were semi-detached with three bedrooms, so the working classes wouldn't have more than two children – a clever way of controlling population, Mr Skeggs remarked.

Skeggs' house had a little black chimney pot on top like a top hat. "It's so sweet," I whispered to Skeggs on the way in and she'd winced. A living room, a small kitchen, two tiny bedrooms, the parents' one large enough for a double bed and a chest of drawers, completed the entire house. When I asked Skeggs where her little sister Tatiana slept, she frowned and I knew I shouldn't have mentioned it. "With my parents," she whispered stiffly. Tatie was still only five. Both Skeggs and her sister had Russian names as befitting the coming revolution, and Skeggs had taken part in choosing Tatiana's, part of the democratic process.

One wall was lined with birdcages, the birds in them blue and green and yellow. "Budgies and canaries," said Skeggs cautiously, not sure of my approval as they fluttered and beat their wings against the bars. "They're hens," she added. "They've not had baby chicks yet."

"Kezia knows Shakespeare, Dad." Skeggs addressed her father in a low voice. He was sitting in his chair by the fire. "She knows whole passages by heart." She knew better than to add "and the psalms". (*Blessed is he that walketh not in the counsel of the ungodly…*)

"Is that so?" said Mr Skeggs in a tight little voice; he had a high, thin, reedy voice for a man. "And is he a good fellow?"

We tittered suitably.

"Well, let's hear yer then."

I was conscious of my lilting Welsh accent, thick and low as I stood before the fire and recited from *A Midsummer Night's Dream.*

"I know a bank where the wild thyme grows
where oxlips and the nodding violet blows.
full-canopied by luscious woodbine
and sweet musk roses and with eglantine…"

I had what Miss Gruffith called "expression".

Mrs Skeggs clapped her hands at the end. "Eee, but that was luvly, Kezia, luv, an' all by heart. Eee but she's a bonny girl, isn't she, Ron?"

Mr Skeggs had a tight little smile on his face. I sensed that perhaps "luscious woodbine" and "musk roses" might not endear themselves to a working man as Ronald Skeggs, perhaps too fanciful and aristocratic.

I switched to "The Pedlar's Caravan", the closest thing I could think of to a landless peasant.

"I wish I lived in a caravan,
with a horse to drive like the pedlar man.
Where he comes from nobody knows…"

"My father approves of you," said Skeggs later, gratified, as she walked home with me up our hill. "He thinks you're intelligent." Which must mean we were friends, and I would accompany her and her father to the next meeting at the Workers' Institute in Swansea, down by the docks, a suitably cold utilitarian place with long red doors, where Mr Skeggs was known as Comrade Skeggs and had once given a talk on slave wages.

***

Skeggs was allowed to visit me in return, "for an hour" she said breathlessly.

I was concerned. Nanny Norman had come for tea; she enjoyed flowers and hot-house tomatoes from Daddy's old glasshouse at the bottom of the garden, to take home. Skeggs would be sure to note that Nanny, with her rows of pearls and marcasite brooch and gracious ways was unmistakably *bourgeoisie* – she owned properties in town, one of which was let, and so was obviously an enemy of the people, as was Granpa. (Dear old Gramps with his waistcoat and gold watch and pint of beer at the Liberal Club where he had a private room, a far call from the Worker's Institute.)

But Skeggs shook Nanny's hand nicely and said, "How do you do, Mrs Withrow-Norman," in her cool accent.

"My grandmother says you're polite," I told Skeggs on the way back to her house. What Nanny had actually said was that for a girl from the prefabs, Olga Skeggs would go far.

More cause for concern was my father who, to my knowledge, had never opened a book in his life. His heroes were cricketers like Compton, his concerns who had scored a century for England in the last test match, and who was going to win the Ashes, England or Australia, all of which Mr Skeggs regarded as a *bourgeois* pastime instigated by the government to keep the workers' minds off their exploitation.

I thought I'd stress Daddy's music collection. "Oh, that's Caruso singing '*Cielo e mar*' from La Gioconda, Act Two," I said airily when Skeggs asked what that noise was in the front room. Skeggs' eyes widened. I imagined her telling her father that Mr Thomas listened to opera; he could belong in one of Stalin's Palaces of Culture. Mr Skeggs, of course, listened to the Red Army Choir on the radio.

But Mother was a different kettle of fish.

She was surely the epitome of the new Soviet woman who went out to work in the world of men on an equal footing, the only mother who did for miles around, striding about the council estate in her long loose slacks, quite unlike Mrs Skeggs. Mother was a secretary for Professor Cruikshank in the Social Science department at the university, which meant she earned money of her own. Mother also smoked and wore bright lipstick and wasn't at home with her children all the time. Everyone on the estate knew that Drusilla and I let ourselves in after school with the key left on the sill of the outside lavatory.

It seemed there had been words one Saturday at the fish stall, Mother towering over Mr Skeggs, demanding the order be weighed again on the scales. Mr Skeggs had snarled, "Get back home to your kids where you belong."

"Back to the division of labour?" Mother had shot back, tossing her head, whereupon Mr Skeggs reportedly had practically flung the piece of cod in her face.

"I shan't be going back there!" Mother had blazed.

She asked Skeggs if she wanted a cup of tea. And I saw Mother, then, dominating, cool, and that Skeggs saw it too. It was Father who was warm and fuzzy and soft, teasing her and calling her Skeggs, thinking it was a nickname.

***

I regularly went home from school with Skeggs and her mother after that. Mrs Skeggs picked up little Tatie from infant school, and we all walked together up the steep hill to the prefab. We had a cup of tea, sitting on the settee by the fire, listening to Mrs Skeggs, who was most voluble about her girlhood in the Worral. She too had been a reader, but of Victorian novels. "Eee, but I luved *Wuthering 'Aights*, Kezia luv!"

Skeggs hovered anxiously round her mother as she switched to the subject of her courtship with Mr Skeggs. "Oh, Mater, *please!*" she said, half chidingly, half affectionately. *Mater* was the word upper-class English boarding-school girls used for "mother" – "the old Mater".

Mrs Skeggs carried on: it seemed that she had been on canteen duty in the army mess hall in her village when she and "our Ron" had met. And you could see that, yes, long ago, one summer during the war, Mrs Skeggs must have been a pretty, silly eighteen-year-old with fluttering blue eyes and frizzy red hair, and Mr Skeggs a dashing and dark-haired Welsh corporal in his uniform, off for the front. They had danced at the army base and "fallen in luv, Kezia aye!" she sighed.

I gripped my teacup at this, for my parents never acknowledged such things. Mrs Skeggs' eyes were shining, her open mouth smiling at some far-off recollection.

"'E swept me off my feet, aye." – "Oh Mater, *really!*" went Skeggs, agitated.

I envied Skeggs her cosy, untidy home, with its budgies and dog Leo (named for Leo Tolstoy, who had freed all the serfs on his Russian estate and taught them to read and write.)

"That one's a prize budgie." Skeggs pointed proudly at a cage. The bird was green, luminescent, with clipped wings.

"Oh, but isn't that cruel, it won't ever be able to fly!" It was my first hint against her father, against the system.

Skeggs looked startled. "Oh, he does let them out from time to time."

Mr Skeggs got in from the fish at five-thirty sharp, and everything changed. His place was by the fire after he'd washed and changed. "Ron's chair," Mrs Skeggs sighed, and she scurried to get him his slippers and a fresh cup of tea, and his book.

Mr Skeggs was a world expert on Winston Churchill and the Second World War. He was reading through every volume written by Churchill himself for the second time in case he'd missed anything first time through. There were to be six volumes in all; Churchill wasn't finished yet. Mr Skeggs had reached the overthrow of the Tory government by Attlee's Labour party at the end of the war, 26 July 1945: Clement Attlee, a man of impeccable honesty, was sent for by the king, King George VI. "A landslide," chuckled Mr Skeggs. "The power of the British workers in action." (Lord Louis Mountbatten, the Queen's third cousin, had apparently confessed to socialist sympathies.)

"'Im and 'is books, they don't half make my arms ache, carrying them from the Mumbles library," fluttered Mrs Skeggs,

Mr Skeggs had been in the Middle East in the war, fighting with Rommel in Egypt. He consequently suffered from malaria and took quinine. It was why he was so thin, it seemed, and only had half a stomach.

"Yewer father in the war?"

I shook my head and mumbled that my father had been a firefighter in the Home Front. His job at the power station had been deemed an "essential service".

Mr Skeggs nodded. Somebody had to keep the home fires burning, he quipped, keep the coal moving for their capitalist imperialist wars, which seemed a terrible thing to say about our finest hour.

"But my grandfather was gassed in the trenches in the Great War," I proffered.

Mr Skeggs' face twitched. "Cannon fodder, just bloody cannon fodder," he snarled.

He opened a shiny magazine, *Pravda* (The Truth), which he ordered specially from the Soviet Union. Mr Skeggs was teaching himself Russian, for Russia was the place to be, he indicated, turning the pages. Skeggs drew close and looked with pride at pictures of the Bolshoi Ballet and the Red Army Choir. Here was peasant art, a painting of a worker in a tiny lamp-lit hut reading to his little grandson. "It could be us," breathed Skeggs in awe, in the tiny prefab by the glow of the fire. Mrs Skeggs brought in the small tin bath for Tatie's nightly sponge in front of the fire. I tried not to look shocked as Mr Skeggs himself, with a chuckle, lifted naked Tatiana, squealing delightedly, into the water – Mrs Skeggs had brought in kettles of hot water earlier – and watched Tatie splash and gurgle and spread her chubby legs. "Dada!" This must be the revolutionary way of family life, freedom of the sexes.

Skeggs watched, hunched beside the settee, and I watched Skeggs. For an evolutionary process of my own had been taking place inside me, a silent, intimate, inevitable force, as I'd started menstruating; the first trickle I'd suspected would happen, that I'd heard about from the other girls who had older sisters, in the secret pre-adolescent world.

Mr Skeggs had Tatie, wrapped in a towel, cuddled in his lap for a while. "That's my little girl," he squeaked in his reedy little voice, fondling her as she giggled and snuggled into him. Finally, Mrs Skeggs took her and put her in their bed in the other room.

It was winter, a drizzly cold mist pressing against the window pane. Mr Skeggs took up Gogol's *House of the Dead*.

Mother Russia took care of her workers. There were Palaces of Culture right on factory sites, explained Mr Skeggs: a worker need go no further. The blocks of flats were also built right on site next to the palace that contained the worker's every need: a skating rink, sports complex including a fifty-metre pool, free day-care with the best books and educational toys available. (Of course, this was long before Stalin's death and the revelation of the great purges, his own houses of the dead – was it five or fifty million workers perished in the Soviet death camps under Stalin's "iron rule"?)

The Leninsky plant, named for Lenin, father of the 1917 Bolshevik Revolution, had day-care and twenty-four classes in folk dancing, gymnastics and ballet, Mr Skeggs resumed. The Summer Palace of Peter the Great in Leningrad (now St Petersburg) had been opened for the use of the workers, he stressed, which was surely what King George VI up in London should be doing with Buckingham Palace.

Then the king died in his sleep. It was 5 February 1952, a dreary wet day. *"The king is dead!"* went the radio broadcaster on the BBC network and the Welsh Programme, repeated every half hour. They played the Dead March all day, a sombre tune, and all the neighbours, except the Skeggses, kept their curtains drawn for three days. I was relieved to hear Daddy say, "So the king is dead. Makes no bloody difference to my life," as he pulled on his wellington boots to go get pats of cow manure from the common for mulch. He was annoyed that all the sports newscasts on the radio were cancelled.

There was a picture on the front page of the *South Wales Evening Post* of the three queens dressed in black, with black veils over their faces, standing in Westminster Hall for the king's Lying-in-State: the new Queen Elizabeth, her mother, Queen Elizabeth, who had now gone down in rank to "Queen Mother" and would have to bow to her daughter from now on, and old Queen Mary, the king's mother. We workers were not allowed to see their faces. "Damn rot," said Mr Skeggs.

But there was no denying the thrill of the Queen's coming coronation. It took place a year later, on 2 June 1953. Thirty thousand people had camped overnight outside Buckingham Palace in the rain, singing and waiting. Eight hundred and fifty thousand people were in London to watch the procession, for Her Royal Highness was to ride in the Golden State Coach from Buckingham Palace to Westminster Abbey for her coronation at 11:00 a.m., wearing a tiara.

School was closed for the occasion. A national holiday declared. It was all to be televised for the workers, those who sported televisions, for everyone, for the first time in history: the crowning of a British monarch.

Beryl Evans' parents were the only ones on the estate rich enough to own a television. Suddenly, quiet, unobtrusive Beryl was the centre of attention. Mr and Mrs Evans had decided, since it was a historic occasion, to open up their house to Beryl's friends, working-class children of the neighbourhood, to watch the ceremony. Ten of us crammed into the Evanses' living room to view the event, along with the Evans family. We'd already each been given a commemorative coronation plate at school, on which was painted the portraits of Her Royal Highness Elizabeth and Prince Philip (he was now a prince), side by side, smiling forever. We were to hang it on a wall so we'd always remember this day – and be loyal to the monarchy, added Skeggs, with that condescending little smirk on her face, like her father's.

The key question was whether Skeggs would stand for the national anthem when it was played, and participate in the singing of "The Queen". "God save our gracious queen" – neither of which she and her father believed in. She had squeezed into the Evanses' living room with the rest of us, sitting cross-legged on the floor, packed in between Mrs Evans' Welsh dresser and the dining table pushed against the wall, not wanting to miss the fun. It was history, after all, she'd murmured somewhat shamefacedly.

"There are two sides to every question," she fluttered enigmatically. What on earth did she mean?

"Huh, she got that from 'er father," scorned Drusilla. Then we forgot about it in the wonder of the gold coach gliding down the Mall in London, the roars of the crowd, the dainty, restrained way Her Royal Highness waved her hand, just from the wrist.

Soon the screen moved in an entrancing maze of images, of incense and coronets, jewels and ermine-lined furs inside Westminster Abbey, the choirs soaring as the Archbishop of Canterbury, the most important person there, since he was the one allowed to do the mysterious anointing of the new queen's head and breast under a special canopy – so the plebs wouldn't see, hissed Skeggs snarkily – "sh-sh-sh!" The archbishop raised the ancient jewelled crown of St Edward high over Elizabeth's head at the throne, turning north, south, east and west for the proclamation of Elizabeth as Queen of the United Kingdom, which included Wales and Northern Ireland, and the British Commonwealth, six hundred and fifty million people. "Huh!" went Skeggs, turning red, out of loyalty to her father. There was a great shout in the abbey and everyone in the living room rose obediently and faced the new queen on the Evanses' TV screen for the singing of the national anthem, along with the choirs of the abbey and all the lords and peers and countesses, ladies-in-waiting, and little Prince Charles in his stall: "*God save our gracious queen, long live our noble queen. .*"

"Why should *she* be saved?" Mr Skeggs had apparently sneered, according to Skeggs. "What about the workers?" Skeggs twisted her mouth in that supercilious way of hers.

Mrs Evans had tears streaming down her face, and Mr Evans filled our glasses with the sherry he'd been keeping for this day, for the toast. "Once in a lifetime, mun, what the heck!"

We were to proclaim altogether, "To the Queen! Long may she reign!"

We began singing the anthem in English. Now was the moment. Skeggs wavered, swaying to her feet, for how could a good comrade send Her Royal Highness victorious, long to reign over us? She mumbled she had to go to the toilet.

And so she missed the moment of crowning, St Edward's crown lowered over the new queen's head, the burst of singing, and Mr Evans' toast with real wine afterwards, the loud hurrah, everyone saying we kids would never forget this as long as we lived, history in the making. "Hurrah! Hurrah! Long live Queen Elizabeth!" as Skeggs sat huddled out in the lavatory alone, her hands crossed protectively over her new, small breasts.

I raised my glass, but did not drink.

The author and her twin sister age ten.

WHICH ONE ARE YOU?

Mother and Father took pride in treating Drusilla and I equally, as we were twins. We shared, for instance, the sweets ration in the Ration Book – there was still rationing, though the war had been over for several years – one bar of Cadbury's chocolate carefully divided between us, or a twist of liquorice cut in half. The same scooping of porridge for breakfast in identical bowls, with lambs gambolling round the rim.

For our seventh birthday we were each given an identical celluloid doll with celluloid curls and staring blue eyes. We loved those dolls and their rosebud lips. I called mine Elizabeth and Drusilla named hers Margaret Rose, after the princesses in the Royal Family. Elizabeth and Margaret Rose were dressed alike in flowery dresses much like our own, and painted-on shoes. We carried them everywhere in our arms. When Nanny Norman found two dinky plastic doll baby bottles in Woolworth's for us, our joy knew no bounds. Now we could feed our babies. It was interesting how we treated Elizabeth and Margaret Rose in a not unsimilar way to how we'd been treated ourselves.

"Feed time, Mrs Thomas," I'd say to Drusilla. "Elizabeth is hungry."

Drusilla would nod. "I got to give Marg'rit-Rose 'er bottle too."

We pushed the tiny plastic teats through the pin-hole mouths with absolute delight. We bathed them together in a bowl, as Mammy had bathed us. For Christmas our mother gave us a baby brush and comb set each for our dolls, and Aunty Do-Do sent us each an identical little doll's pram.

Only Nanny Thomas – Welsh nangi – on Daddy's side, diverged from the norm.

"Yew the smart one what can already read big books?" She peered at me fiercely over the counter of her sweet shop in Fforestfawr, where Daddy took us every Sunday to visit. She gave me a lovely book, *The Water Babies*, by someone called Charles Kingsley, for my next birthday. The illustration on the cover showed a naked little boy called Tom riding a fish, with seaweed flowing around his head. He was a chimney sweep and had escaped from evil Mr Grimes to the sea, where he now swam freely to his heart's content underwater without drowning. I could already make out hard words like "chimney" and "whale". She gave Drusilla a little dustpan and brush. For the first time, I vaguely sensed I wasn't Drusilla.

We were dressed alike, of course, right down to our liberty bodices and knickers. In winter we wore identical flared skirts, long grey ribbed socks to our knees, and matching jerseys. In summer we flounced around shyly in little dresses with puffed sleeves that must have taken Mammy ages to sew at night on the Singer sewing machine. Matching bows perched on our heads like two limp birds. "Ooh, ain't they *lovely*," everyone cooed wherever we went. "*Twins!*" they'd marvel, as if we'd descended hand in hand from the clouds. People – invariably women – gave us money. "Here, here's sixpence, dears," one old lady smiled creepily at us on the Mumbles train. She had a black, worn handbag over her arm, with a brass clasp, and she actually pressed a sixpenny bit into each of our palms she surely couldn't afford. "For being twins," she trembled, making me sad, even though sixpence bought an awful lot of liquorice and sherbet at Dan's Variety.

"There go the Thomas twins!" neighbours would echo, which I hated, as Drusilla and I walked down Linden Hill together, dressed in identical little homemade velvet coats and matching bonnets at Whitsun. Who was I, always attached to this other little girl? I'd turn around and there was my other self, Drusilla, in her white lisle socks and button-down patent shoes just like mine, and her row of silly ringlets.

"Now, which twin are you?" neighbours would ask. Worse, "Which one are you?" It particularly infuriated me as I sidled past Mrs Rees and Mrs Harris and Mrs Matthews gossiping around Mrs Harris' front gate. They'd stare as if trying to figure me out.

"Is it Kezia or Drusilla?"

"Oh I thinks it's Drusilla, Jean; look at the eyes." This only enraged me more. It wasn't as if I really closely resembled my sister, who had a round baby-face and bluish eyes. I had darker fair hair and *brown* eyes. Couldn't these neighbours see straight?

"*This one* grinds her teeth," said Dr Morton, the school dentist on public health examination day in Mumbles School, poking my molars with a steel pick. Was it any wonder? Pupils were called out of class one at a time to be examined, but of course Drusilla and I were called out together to go to the office.

"The Thomas twins next," droned Miss Davis from her high desk, as if we were glued together.

Was it any wonder I didn't know who I was until age eleven; I mean as a separate human being?

I wasn't even sure I really liked Drusilla, though I didn't as yet realise that. She'd push me aside to be first to get the front seat upstairs on the double-decker bus, as if it was her right. It hadn't been a surprise when she'd snatched the Union Jack out of my hand on VE Day, celebrating the "end of the war", that Mammy – or was it Nanny? – had just given me. "Here, wave this, Kezia, the war is over!" she'd cried, in tears. It was the only flag left on the street. We'd been told to share, as we were twins. "You'll have to share," I came to understand, was a subtle nod to Drusilla to grab everything for herself – the Union Jack that day (we were supposed to "share nicely"), the spinning top only she spun until she tired of it, then I'd get my turn. I could go on and on.

"They play so *nicely* together," Mammy cooed to the neighbours, which might have been the beginning of a secret life-long desperation I seemed to carry inside. That word "nice" again.

"Drusilla is so sunny-natured!" people said, with implications about me. True, all the child photos of us together – "Put your arms around each other nicely, now", *click* – show me frowning, anxious and bewildered. "Drusilla took my penny," fell on deaf ears. Mammy just couldn't seem to hear anything against Drusilla, as if it were unfair somehow because, after all, I was the smart one in school. I seized on it pathetically: so I *was* different, then.

***

Drusilla was stealing money out of Mammy's purse again. We were about ten by then.

"You're stealing from Mammy!" I cried.

"Well, she doesn't count 'er change," Drusilla retaliated as if I were a dimwit.

I had to think about that, about this new morality Drusilla presented. If it was our mother's fault she didn't count her money, then that meant Drusilla was not to blame for taking a sixpence. (It was therefore not stealing.)

But when I stole geraniums out of Mrs Jinks' window box next door, I got a good hiding. Mrs Jinks wore a big, cotton, shapeless dress covered in faded flowers over her roly-poly body. She shuffled around the back garden, but the window box was in the front window, out of her vision. But Mrs Evans on the other side of the road had seen one of the Thomas twins stealing, and told Mrs Jinks. "I don't know which one of them it was, they looks the same." Daddy said he'd handle it.

"Did yew steal geraniums out of Mrs Jinks' window-box, Kezia?"

"Just a few, Dad… there was lots there," I hedged, using Drusilla's moral compass. If there were lots then I wasn't really stealing, was I?

"Never mind lots," snarled Daddy. "Yew was *stealing*, that's wrong."

Daddy spanked me hard in front of Mrs Jinks, who went red in the face and looked away. I think she felt a bit guilty, but nevertheless exonerated and virtuous. She went inside. She regarded Drusilla as "a much nicer child". Kezia Thomas was not to be trusted. She was the brazen one who had stolen geraniums right out of her window box.

***

One day, everything changed. The headmaster, Mr Rudge, summonsed our parents to the school for an interview. It transpired that Drusilla and I were to be separated in the coming year in standard three. I was placed in 3A, the smart stream, and Drusilla into 3B, the slower one – "where she belonged," Mr Rudge had apparently said sensibly. We'd never been separated before. Twins were kept together in school out of psychological necessity. Who knew what would happen to their brains if parted? That was the thinking of the day, which Mammy and Daddy trusted.

Of course our parents did not tell us; they kept it to themselves at first. I overheard Mammy complaining to Nanny about it the following Saturday morning – Drusilla had gone out to the outside lavatory to pee. Mammy was saying in a low tone, "He said Kezia is very intelligent, top of the class." Something I'd never known, since Mammy never let us see our reports at the end of each term, to protect Drusilla. "It's for their own good, he said."

I couldn't hear Nanny's response, but I heard her say to her friend Mrs Perman another time when she was minding us, "It don't do for girls to be too clever, Elvira," and Mrs Perman agreed.

"Didn' do me no 'arm, Emmie, to only go to standard five. Then I met Wilf."

But I thrilled: Mr Rudge had verified the Thomas twins *were* different, despite the silly identical bows in our hair.

Drusilla suspected something was up, of course; her face developed that tight, rebellious, betrayed look, her lips screwed into a thin line. Mammy and Daddy had to be careful when the moment came to take her aside to explain things. I'd hear them whispering. Did Drusilla hear the whispers too? She must have.

Still, nothing was said outright. I'd always understood in a vague way that of course Mammy and Daddy couldn't ever praise me or show off my report at the end of term and say "You've done well, Kezia, top of the class." It would be terribly insensitive. It would be cruel. Now I didn't know what gentle words they used to soften the blow to Drusilla's self-esteem. But Nanny Thomas made no bones about it; she had no such scruples.

Drusilla scowled at Nanny Thomas when she leaned over her sweet counter in her shop on our Sunday morning visit and said delightedly, "Which one is the clever one, then? It's Kezia." She called Drusilla "the dull one". To her face.

"I dun' like you," Drusilla dared to shoot back, shocking me. She snatched her ice cream out of Nanny Thomas' trembling hand. But nothing happened to her. If anything, she was admired for it.

"That Drusilla!" cackled Nanny Thomas. "She's a one."

So which one was I? Not daring, not retaliatory – that prospect always terrified me.

"You're a sap!" said Drusilla, and she gave me a push, but I didn't push her back because the new status quo had implicitly bewildered us both. I was top of the class and poor Drusilla was at the bottom, which gave her a lot of freedom, in a way, I'd reflect with some envy. The freedom not to care, and she didn't.

***

The first day of school that September we were separated, for the first time in our lives. I was now in Miss Woolley's class, and Drusilla in Miss Vernon's. We hung up our coats in the girls' cloakroom: rows and rows of coats and scarves, with rows of little wellingtons underneath. Drusilla trailed after me across the great centre hall, perhaps out of curiosity or, worse, perhaps thinking – hoping? – she might be in Miss Woolley's class after all and there'd been a mistake; she'd always been with me.

"You can't come in." I turned to her at Miss Woolley's dreaded door – she was the terror of the school, even the headmaster was in awe of her.

"Ugh! Dun' want to! Miss Woolley's old an' ugly." Drusilla spat out the words. Her mouth curled in a triumphant sneer as she saw the shock on my face. "Miss Vernon's pretty!"

I saw what Drusilla was doing, I'd always seen, but for once I didn't care. I was delirious with excitement and anxiety: I was to be on my own even though our mother still dressed us in identical skirts and jumpers, same colour, and those idiotic bows in our hair. I was going to be free of Drusilla.

But the strange thing was that we still existed in a sort of seesaw comparison of each other: I was in the strict class, which seemed to mean high standards, while Drusilla was in the "easy" class with lax Miss Vernon. I had to sit up straight at all times at my desk, eyes transfixed on Miss Woolley at her high desk in the corner; the great, majestic yet kind Miss Woolley. I loved it; I loved strictness and rules and awe and obedience. Knowing your place (at last).

I liked it that everyone was terrified of Miss Woolley, and I was in her class. "You're in *Miss Woolley's* class?" Awe and grudging admiration. "Aren't you *scared*?"

There were inkwells in each desk and straight-nib pens in the runnels. I thought how wonderful it was to be sitting there without Drusilla's mournful, defiant face at the other end of the classroom. She'd always sat in the bottom row – for we sat in order of ability for the teacher to see who the smart ones were, something we never questioned. Somehow I had been offended by Drusilla's presence, forever suffocated by the image of the Thomas twins. Now I sat by myself, Kezia Thomas, hands folded, loving Miss Woolley; she was my beloved teacher. There was a special row of desks Miss Woolley drew our attention to that first week, which did not face the board but sat sideways to the class. "That's the zoo!" said Miss Woolley, amused. She rapped the ruler against her desk. "That's where the duffers go. Dumbo the elephant, Suzie snail, Alfie ape…" She had names for all the sad unfortunates who failed in their work, came bottom in spelling tests, or could not do mental arithmetic, who did not excel, did not *listen*. I shuddered: it was obvious that was where Drusilla would have belonged, in shame, and I felt a melancholy stab of horror for her, *No!* rising up.

Then Drusilla came knocking on Miss Woolley's door first thing Friday morning that first week with my dinner money in hand. Mammy didn't trust me to carry my own – ten shillings and sixpence for a week's school dinners; I'd be sure to lose it. "She's such a drippy drawers, just like Aunty Dora," she'd say to no one in particular. I'd always lost things: the bangle that just disappeared off my arm in the schoolyard when I was five, pennies that disappeared from my pockets, hair ribbons that just flew out of my hair without anyone seeing. Once, a brand-new identical blue blazer Mammy bought us, one each, in the market. I'd lost mine in five minutes. It just slipped from my arm, I wasn't sure how – I didn't recollect even putting it on. I'd gaped up at Mammy, bewildered. A new blazer? What blazer? Tears filled my eyes. "YOU'VE GONE AND LOST YOUR NEW BLAZER!" Mammy was screaming in disbelief in front of all sorts of women doing their shopping at the stalls. "ALL OUR CLOTHING COUPONS, GONE!"

I shook my head, I couldn't believe it either, but it was undeniable. Kezia the drip had lost a blazer minutes after it being bought for her, and it had cost four pounds.

"FOUR POUNDS!" Mammy kept shrieking, hysterical.

Drusilla, who of course was sensibly wearing hers, smirked. So now I definitely was not to be trusted with something so precious as ten shillings and sixpence dinner money, even two years later at age nine. Drusilla never lost anything, certainly not shillings and sixpences. She had something I didn't: what the grown-ups called common sense.

"What are you doing knocking on my door?" Miss Woolley had left her revered high seat and stomped over to the door after calling the register. She opened it. There stood Drusilla, mouth pursed, unfazed. She said, matter-of-factly, "Mammy said I got to give my sister Kezia 'er dinner money."

"Oh Mammy did, did she? Well, tell Mammy that from now on Kezia Thomas carries her own dinner money to school on a Friday. And I don't want to see you at my door again."

Slam. Miss Woolley had glanced back at my face, shrunk down in shame at my desk, and grasped the picture.

"Dun' like that Miss Woolley anyway! She's ugly!" cried Drusilla, vehemently. Enjoying the shock on my face every time at her fearlessness. She saw through something I could not about adults.

It was as if, at last, we weren't twins as much as we used to be; we were beginning to think differently. Drusilla seemed to have *opinions*, every now and again. She knew she was separated from me and why. She never said a word about Miss Vernon and what it was like being in her class. It was none of my business.

But I knew she could loll about all she pleased in her seat in class, and even change desks to be with a different girl if she wanted; Miss Vernon didn't seem to mind. They did things like crayoning and cutting out patterns with little school-board scissors because too much arithmetic and writing was stressful for that kind of pupil. Miss Vernon was of the opinion they needed to "work with their hands". This was the first time we heard this concept, "manual work", "working with your hands" (instead of your brains was the implicit message, that suddenly applied to Drusilla. No wonder she hated school).

So Drusilla was with lax, cheerful, slightly dotty Miss Vernon who had dyed blonde curls and wore lipstick and apparently said fanciful things like "Oh I *do* love the sound of a lawnmower outside, harbinger of spring!" Mrs Vernon did things like throw the windows wide open to the fresh air to let in the scent of the fresh-mown grass, while Miss Woolley had Arthur Jones pull the sash and open the lower part of the windows a tad, not to let in wasps.

Once a week we had exchange afternoons, when half of the girls in A class crossed over to Miss Vernon's room for "raffia work", and half the girls in B class came to Miss Woolley's for needlework and knitting. The boys went to Mr Wilks for woodwork. There was quite an excitement and fuss in the classroom, pulling out boxes of threads and cards of needles and bundles of wool in readiness. The teachers must have put some thought into what to do with the

Thomas twins, for Drusilla and I were never in the same half, and as I passed her by in the hall with my group, her face was tight and pinched at the thought of an afternoon of knitting with the ogre.

I began to feel a vague sort of shame at Drusilla being separated from me like this. There was a loss; she wasn't there, and I suppose she had been used to me being in the room even if it had been rows ahead of her. She must have known in her heart why Mammy and Daddy kept her report card from her, children know. Sitting in Miss Vernon's class in the sunlight, twisting raffia into dolls, I had the sensation of being Drusilla and what it must be like for her in her new class, and she would have seen what it was like for me in strict Miss Wooley's class; but not a word was said between us.

After school we no longer met up in the lobby and walked home together as we were supposed to; there was a chasm. Drusilla went off defiantly with Connie Oskins, and that was when we were no longer twins. We would never walk home from school together again; had we but known it, we'd drifted apart, Mammy's great fear. Instead, I walked quickly by myself so no one – Drusilla – could catch up with me, along the seafront following the Mumbles train track round the bay, and then the long trek up Linden Hill. I let myself into the house with the big iron key that was left on the windowsill of the outside lavatory. The window was small, of glazed green glass which let in an eerie greenish light. For a moment I stood bewildered and alarmed, fearful of the cold empty lavatory attached to the back kitchen, and the empty house that was dreary without anybody home – Mammy was still at work. I was suddenly sorry Drusilla didn't walk with me anymore. I had to wait. Tentatively I put on a light, first in the kitchen and then in each room I passed through: the hall light, the living-room light.

"What's all these lights on for?" Daddy would say heavily when he came in from shift, switching them off. I didn't say because I was frightened of the dark house. "Where's yewer sister? Yew supposed to come 'ome together."

I pretended not to know. I did know that Drusilla sneaked off to Connie Oskins' house on the estate, not because of Connie but because of Mrs Oskins, who I'd heard made a big fuss of Drusilla. Mrs Oskins lay around on her sofa and was rumoured not to wear anything under her skirt, no panties, nothing. I heard this from some of the girls going home, snickering. It was shocking and disturbing – what did Mrs Oskins mean by not covering that part? Did Drusilla *see*? (Was that why she went there?)

"My Ma *loves* yewer sister," said Connie in the schoolyard, in a nasal whine. I wouldn't want to be friends with her. She was in 3B with Drusilla; she didn't care about school and talked back at Miss Vernon in class and she was only ten. I recalled how Drusilla stood in the schoolyard at home time in her worn wool skirt and woolly jumper pulling tight across her shoulders, her hair bunched up in that crooked, ferocious bow, waiting for Connie. Not a backward glance for me, taking off with her friend, the sort of girl Mammy would have a fit about if she knew (but she didn't know). Connie Oskins was what Mammy would call a bad influence, a phrase she used of certain kids around the council estate. Perhaps she did know about Drusilla going to the Oskins' place.

I think then that Mr Rudge putting us in separate classes, for Drusilla to have those raffia lessons with dotty, free-thinking Miss Vernon, somehow signified more than the mere divide between us. Did Mammy sense that? She sensed something, some imminent though as yet far-off danger that would emerge in our teens. Mammy told Mrs Goddard she knew Drusilla wasn't smart in school so she wanted Drusilla at least to have "nice" friends, meaning ones who did not drop their *h*s and did well in school. Mrs Goddard, sitting on our settee (Daddy was at work), smoking madly, agreed; and I think Drusilla knew that, that Mammy was out to improve her, which meant of course there must be something wrong with her. (Drusilla wasn't stupid, far from it.)

Suddenly, one day, it seemed Mammy had signed up Drusilla for elocution lessons with Madame Katerina, the best and oldest elocutionist in Swansea. Mammy herself had gone to her as a girl, which must be why she had such lovely clear diction. (What had Nanny had in view for Mammy, her elder daughter?) I sat out in the waiting room on an old antimacassar chair while Drusilla went in with Mammy for her first lesson. Madame Katerina was big and heavy, her face thick with beige powder and a streak of lipstick.

Madame Katerina sounded formidable. "She got a big mouth," Drusilla pronounced after the first lesson.

"*She's*," Mammy corrected, and Drusilla pulled a face and sulked.

Madame Katerina said: "Make your vowels *round*, Drusilla, watch and listen to me." And she opened her mouth big enough to swallow you whole, grumbled Drusilla afterwards. "Open your *mouth,* Drusilla. Release those aspirates, I want to hear that *h.*- Huh huh huh." That was to stop Drusilla slurring her vowels and dropping her *h*s, make her speak *distinctly* with an upper-class accent, like Princesses Elizabeth and Margaret and their mother, the Queen, which was after all what Mammy was paying for.

"You can't make a pig's whistle out of a sow's ear, Mavis," said Nanny obliquely one Saturday, and Mammy got mad.

But I was terribly excited and impressed. I watched with adulation and some envy for the results in Drusilla's diction, the change for the better in her Welsh accent that I'd never actually thought was something that needed changing, but was soon to be transformed into the thin, dulcet tones of the Royal Family. I was going to have a twin sister who spoke like nails being scraped across a blackboard. "Ew-w, rarelly?" ("Oh really?") For the first time I saw some possible honour in being a twin to Drusilla. But Drusilla sounded much like ever before, whining "Dun' wanna…" for "Don't want to." I realised then that not only Drusilla but our father didn't fulfil the aspirations of Madame Katerina. I knew, sadly, from Madame Katerina's reputed drills, that poor Daddy dropped his vital aspirate, calling Mrs Harris down the hill "Mrs 'Arris".

"Oh! Who *cares*!" cried Drusilla suddenly, turning on me, her face very red and fierce. She ran out to play in the street with all the kids, our friends for a long time: Betty Morgan, Trisha Morris, Maggie. Madame Katerina gradually drifted from our lives; we forgot about her.

"Oh well…!" said Mammy, tossing off her disappointment.

All the same, a piano appeared in the front room. A bronze, second-hand upright with a faded treble clef scroll on the front, bought from Wilks' Music Shop on Oxford Street in Swansea. Mammy and Aunty Do-Do had grown up with the Wilks sisters; they'd gone to school together before the war. This made the piano special. At once, Mammy sat down and began to play. We never knew Mammy could. Her face was flushed pink and her eyes sparkled. A smile played on her face; she was *another person*, a younger self. Was she a grammar school girl again, back in Nanny and Granpa's old house where she and Aunty Dora – called Do-Do – had grown up?

Her long work-ridden fingers spread across the keys. She was thumping grandly a wonderful piece she said was Mozart's "*Rondo alla Turca*". "Oh, it's been years!" she cried.

Daddy came in from the garden in his overalls and he grinned hugely. "Oh God, Mavis is playing!" He was happy.

Mammy ignored him. She was playing the piece by heart, from memory, her fingers rippling and rattling up and down the keys; she ended with a powerful chord. "There! It all came back to me." Mozart's "*Rondo alla Turca*".

Drusilla and I were beside ourselves. "Oh play another one!" I begged. "You're a wonderful pianist, Mammy!"

Our mother flushed, pleased and flattered.

"Well, I *used* to be good," she said, affecting modesty. "Let's see if I remember Ketèlbey." And she played "Bells Across the Meadow", going back how many years, maybe to when she was twelve or thirteen?

Drusilla went boasting all over the street that we now had a piano: to Betty James and Dotty Morgan, and especially Trisha; the whole of the Mumbles must have known by nightfall that the Thomas twins had a piano. "We got a piano and we're having lessons."

"Wanna see it," Betty James demanded. "Seein' is believing."

Drusilla invited everyone to our house at number 9. Drusilla wanted to charge a penny for a look. In silence, the girls, Dotty,

Betty and Trisha, tiptoed into the kitchen. They looked at everything in passing – our tall tin cupboards, the counter with dishmop in an old jam jar, the tea caddy, the gas stove with its flint hanging on a string – then down the hall, which had a clock ticking on the wall, and finally our front room. There against the wall was the Thomas twins' piano, with the lid up, revealing glittering white keys. I did not know what the black ones were for, something I would learn no doubt from my piano teacher in due course.

"Ooh, there's lovely, aye," everyone agreed, and crowded closer. Betty pressed a key and it rang out. "Oh!"

Each girl had a turn pressing the keys while Drusilla and I watched proudly.

"Let Trisha play something!" But before she could, there was sudden thumping upstairs, and Daddy came down the stairs, red in the face and bristling, dressed in his rumpled pyjamas. We'd forgotten he was on night shift, which meant he had to go to bed during the day to get his sleep. "What the 'ell are you kids doing in here when a man's trying ter get some sleep?"

A moment of shame that neither piano lessons nor elocution with Madame Katerina could exonerate.

Of course Drusilla had to have lessons first. ("Me! Me! Mammy!") when Mammy said, "Now, who wants to learn? Only one of you can have lessons at a time." I resigned myself, knowing I would just have to wait, patiently, for Drusilla's turn to be up.

Mammy gave Drusilla five shillings each week to put in her purse for safekeeping, to give to Mrs Hopkins, the piano teacher Mammy had found. She lived in *Sea View* in the Mumbles, round by the congregational chapel. It was a long, dark street of low brick houses joined together in a row, with tiny squares of gardens in front bordered by a low concrete wall. The lessons were every Thursday. Now that it was an actuality, Drusilla did not seem thrilled to have to go to a piano lesson after school, instead of playing with her friends. She was to go to Mrs Hopkins' house straight after the bell.

"Show me what you learned," I said with excitement, after we'd played "Chopsticks" on the piano together, which any kid could do and got on people's nerves. "Where's 'C'?" I wanted to know. That mythical all-important key. "Middle C is the basis of all piano," Mammy had said in her authoritative way. It was where you placed your hands to start, and I wanted Drusilla to show me so I'd know in advance. I hoped to do well at piano.

"Now don't go taking over," Mammy called sharply from the dining room. "Taking over", "pushing in" on Drusilla was her way of saying "Don't outshine your sister; let Drusilla have a chance to shine at something for a change." It was unfair of me to be learning piano at the same time, she meant, there'd be comparison.

There was anger beneath Mammy's voice and a frustration I didn't understand. I curled up on the couch, deflated.

Drusilla never did show me 'C' or how to do the scales (it never occurred to me she didn't know). Somehow the lessons dwindled in importance. One day towards the end of term, when the sun streamed over the sea at the return of summer and the storms were over, when the waves rose twenty feet in the air and lashed the Mumbles train as it trundled by, Mammy received a letter from Mrs Hopkins. It seemed Drusilla had not attended piano lessons for a long time, did Mrs Thomas want her to pick it up again in the autumn? It turned out Drusilla had been spending the five shillings Mammy had been giving her each Thursday on ice cream and sweets after school, treating her friends, instead of on "The Teddy Bears' Picnic" in the key of C. Now Drusilla would get it. I tensed in anticipation of what Mammy would say in her outrage, for surely such it would be. But not a word of reproach.

"Well, she smelled awful, Mammy, her breath *stank*!" Drusilla said defiantly by way of explanation. There was something familiar about this logic, her lips pursed at being found out.

I looked anxiously at our mother, waiting, longing for the words that would confirm my turn for lessons, but Mammy turned away. I didn't want to *ask*, I wanted mammy to *offer*. Perhaps I already sensed not to put her on the spot, that she was in a predicament, a sort of anguish at stake here.

I wasn't going to have lessons. The next day the piano was gone. When we got in from school I gasped. "Oh, why?"

I knew why, of course. Drusilla's face tightened and she pursed her mouth as usual in that tight way and looked wide-eyed at me in shock. "Oh well, it's done now." Mammy said, and she shrugged, tossing her head; but for one moment she'd looked guilty.

I went outside and hid. It was raining. Presently I heard Daddy's troubled voice coming through the outside wall from the kitchen. "What the 'ell is Kezia doin' by 'erself crying out in the coal-'ouse?"

**

Our mother had left school at fourteen, and her piano lessons had ended then. Maybe Nanny didn't see any point in wasting more money on her (the way Nanny often talked about girls' education) now that Mavis was learning shorthand and typing, and earning money in a job. Mammy joined the Cycling Club and met Daddy, so she had a boyfriend (Daddy) as well. What did she want to be playing Mozart rondos for? Mammy would tell us these stories on a rainy afternoon, giggling to herself on the sofa, and we loved listening. I thought I could detect a level of resentment in Mammy, even anger, at being taken out of school early. (Though lots of girls then left school at fourteen, which seemed unbelievable to me now, even shocking, having to leave school forever in standard three in grammar school.) Mammy had excelled at St Helen's Girls School, which still stood behind Victoria Park, a nice part of Swansea, much nicer than the Sandfields where Nanny and Granpa lived, where she and Aunty Do-Do grew up.

"I played Portia in *The Merchant of Venice*." Mammy's eyes were glistening as she smoked. She waved her cigarette and quoted: *"The quality of mercy is not strained, it falleth like the gentle dew from heaven…"* I didn't really know what that was but it sounded wonderful; I knew Shakespeare was someone very important in English, his plays were written in poetry. The rain fell in sheets outside, beating the front window. Mammy had a fire going; it was part of her memories.

"Shakespeare!" I echoed, impressed.

"Oh yes, Miss Hedwyn said I could have been an actress," Mammy sighed.

I thrilled, I knew Mammy would have been a wonderful actress and said so. Drusilla looked scornful; an *actress*? I could imagine what Nanny would have had to say to that and I sensed for the first time how like Nanny Drusilla was.

A smile played on Mammy's lips when she said "Miss Hedwyn", and it brought back the way I had loved Miss Woolley in standard three in the church school. I loved hearing about Miss Hedwyn and Mammy's schooldays and the special dresses Nanny made her each year for her to attend the Doctors' Hospital Ball in Swansea, the thrill, the excitement, Mammy in a soft frilly pale rose organza (one of her dresses), another year a blue satin, the implication being she would meet and marry a "better sort of man" (not Daddy), maybe a doctor or educated man. But it was her sister Dora – Aunty Do-Do – who had done that, or so it seemed. Dora had married an Englishman from Kent, Clyde Farley. She met him during the war on the coast at Dover during an air raid; she had joined the WAAFs – which meant Women's Auxiliary Air Force – where she had done canteen work making meals for the airmen and packing food for pilots, which used to amuse Nanny since Do-Do couldn't boil an egg. (Imagine Do-Do working in the big wartime munitions factories checking pistons or something for the Bren guns, Nanny would say, amused at the very thought. Or putting screws into munitions without blowing the place up and screaming her head off during the air raids over the coasts of England. Yet she had. She had carried out her responsibilities in Britain's hour of need, I reflected.) Clive Farley had been in the Royal Air Force, working in Morse code and wireless operations. He'd gone to private school and learned French (which meant he was far superior to poor Daddy, a different class altogether). "He has such a mar-r-velous sense of humour, mama!" Aunty Do-Do had apparently written excitedly in a letter to Nanny and Granpa (who was alive then), the Luftwaffe dropping bombs everywhere from the skies over Folkstone. Mammy imitated Aunty Do-Do's silly voice at that time: Aunty Do-Do in love in the WAAF, Aunty Do-Do ringing home after VE Day, "Mama, we're *engaged!*" Nanny had scoffed. "A sense of humour don't put food on the table. What was his job after demobilisation?" Nanny did not approve of Clyde Farley. He put on a lot of swank, she scorned, "And he doesn't have two ha'pennies to rub together." But that was dippy Dora for you, rushing off and getting wed because of a man's *sense of humour*.

But we all loved Aunty Do-Do. She came sometimes to Swansea, from Kent in the south of England, to visit, staying with Nanny and "leaving her useless husband behind", as Nanny put it. The dark middle room seemed to fill with sunlight. Aunty Do-Do was tall like Mammy and had a huge smile and a head thick with woolly curls. "Beautiful hair, Dora always had!" sighed Mammy. Mammy changed. It was wonderful how she became a different person around Dora. Now why was that?

We'd gone to Nanny's house to see Aunt Do-Do. She was sitting in the middle room with Nanny by the fire, and Drusilla and I came in shyly. We didn't know what to expect; we'd been smaller when we last saw her, years back and now we were eleven. No one usually took notice of us or kissed or hugged us, but Aunty Do-Do did. She gave us a hug and said how we'd grown – she noticed – and what lovely girls we were and she could tell us apart now, wasn't Kezia's hair getting darker and Drusilla's hair more curly? For a moment, Nanny and Mammy started; we were still in identical dresses with slides in our hair. But then we were forgotten and Mammy and Do-Do laughed and joked at childhood memories. They called each other "kiddo".

"Hey, kiddo, remember when you cut off every badge from my Guide uniform that time out of spite?"

"Oh!" screamed Aunty Do-Do. "I hid in the bathroom and locked the door, I was so terrified of Mama!" (That would be

Nanny) "I wouldn't come out." Then she'd listened, and when footsteps had gone, she sneaked out and crept up the attic stairs off the landing to escape. She'd climbed, still terrified, out through the skylight and got stuck on the roof. Granpa had to call the fire brigade.

"Laugh! What a drip!" Nanny had joined in the talk too, she enjoyed a laugh. It seemed like a family sport, teasing – ridiculing – Aunty Do-Do, when she and Mammy were girls, for Do-Do's ridiculousness.

"Remember when Dora came home from that Temperance Evangelical meeting down by the gas works? She stood in the middle room and announced, 'Mama! I'm SAVED! I've found JESUS!' Laugh! We nearly died laughing, I think I wet my pants," went Nanny. "Was he lost?"

What a dope! Dopey Dora, Drippy-drawers, believing everything down at the Temperance Hall, not an ounce of common sense. Aunty Do-Do just smiled good-naturedly, going along with the teasing, letting them have their way. But somehow I felt sad. The Salvation Army band still came along Western Street on a Sunday afternoon, the soldiers of Christ playing trumpets and drums, marching along singing "*Onward Christian Soldiers*!" I'd want to join in too and march and salute to Jesus. If Drusilla and I were visiting Nanny, we'd run out on to the street and I'd shout "The band! The band!" I'd be beside myself with joy and Nanny would call bewildered down the passage, "What band? What's she excited about now?" And she was amazed, concerned about me; it was just the Sally Army from the Territorials down Argyle Street, she said, worried I was going to end up like Dora , getting excited over nothing. Do-Do's head had been full of romance that never got her anywhere, she warned, even if she had gone to De la Beche high school.

Something dawned, quite stunning. Drusilla was not even listening, not paying attention; she understood clearly that Aunt Do-Do was dippy. Yet, it seemed, Aunty Do-Do the dip-stick had passed scholarship in her day; she'd won a place in the girls' county high school on De la Beche Road. She would have worn the special uniform and a panama hat with the school's crest on the brim, and learned French and Latin, and stayed until age sixteen. And Mammy had not. I felt a sharp pain; it wasn't fair, I wanted to cry! Mammy had been Portia in *The Merchant of Venice* at St Helen's School, which I now realised was not a grammar school at all but a board school for girls who had failed scholarship, and were destined for Woolworth's or office work, shorthand typists. But when I pressed Aunty Do-Do about it, admiringly, especially the dark blue tunic and striped tie, she just tossed it off. "De la Beche? Oh *that*!" As if being a grammar school girl was no big thing, a fantasy you read about in books. "And don't you believe the half of it in books, Kezia!" Aunty Do-Do swayed in her ratty old cardigan and loose serge skirt and woollen stockings – not an ounce of makeup, noted Nanny. So fey. Or was she being tactful, self-effacing, for Mammy's sake? To save Mammy's face? It was all so long ago, after all.

Dusk was falling outside in Nanny's yard, soft as a moth's wing.

DO YOU SPEAK WELSH?

I was fourteen when I decided to switch from German to Welsh at the girls' county grammar school. I'd been taking German for a week.

There was amazement, expostulations all round. I was sent at once to Miss Hodge, the headmistress, who said, did I know what I was doing? Welsh was a dead language. German was important: the language of industry, philosophy, science and physics, not to mention opera. ("Imagine *Fidelio* sung in Welsh!") Miss Hodge gave a derisive little smile. She had blue-tinted hair as older women did then in the fifties, ironed into waves, and a firm bosom. But I was determined. Welsh was our national language, I said quite boldly for a third-former, adding recklessly, "*Cymru am byth!*" – Wales forever! I was quoting Miss Olwen Glynhower, senior Welsh mistress at the school, who did get carried away at times with her sword at the school eisteddfod on St David's Day. Miss Hodge stiffened. I sensed my mistake; Miss Glynhower was not one of Miss Hodge's more favoured teachers.

She raised an eyebrow. "That's all very well, Kezia, but in the real world you'll find Welsh will get you nowhere. Who on earth speaks it?"

At home, in the kitchen that evening, my father expressed a similar view though in a slightly different vernacular. "Who the 'ell would she talk Welsh to?" he said of me, digging his fork into a lamb chop. "Nobuddy speaks it."

"Nangi does," I said hopefully. "I can talk to Nangi."

Mother stopped stirring the chips in the pan, in disbelief. "*Nangi?* Who's that?"

My sister Drusilla tittered. "I always told you Kezia's not all there."

Nangi, or *nanci,* was the Welsh word for grandmother that I now felt indebted to use for our Nanny Thomas on Father's side, to distinguish her from English-speaking Nanny Norman, on Mother's side.

"I never heard her speak Welsh," said Drusilla, staring.

"Well, sometimes she does. She says '*Bore da*' to customers in her shop all the time." Even Drusilla must remember that from primary school lessons. "She says, '*Bore da, beth yw heddiw?*'" *Good morning, how are you today?*

The foreign-sounding words reverberated round the kitchen with its tin cupboards and linoleum floor. Mother looked astonished.

"Aw, that's not real Welsh, mun," drawled my father. He mashed his 'tatoes into the gravy on his plate. "They're just some words she says to the old gents."

Ancient words with a Celtic drama of their own that had a quite different intonation to the cool sound of English or harsh musicality of German.

"*Siaradwch i gymraeg?*" *Do you speak Welsh?* Old Mr Griffiths had turned to Drusilla and me in Nanny Thomas' shop when we were little. He walked to Ravencliff Park for a cup of tea every Sunday morning after chapel, tapping his gold-tipped cane. He'd smiled down at us, Mrs Thomas' little six-year-old granddaughters.

We shook our heads. Our golden ringlets had swung side to side. "We learn it in school." Which, of course, was an oxymoron; a weekly lesson with old Miss Morgan in Mumbles School.

"They only speaks English," Nangi had said, not without a certain trace of pride.

"We know the national anthem, Mr Griffiths," I'd volunteered.

And so we'd been raised up on one of the glass-topped tables by the counter in Nangi's shop and sung a garbled version of the

Welsh national anthem, usually reserved for rugby matches and St David's Day, the national patron saint day for Wales on March the first.

"*Mae Hen Wlad Fy Nhadau…*" *Old Land of My Fathers*, we'd warbled, faltering, of course, over "*yntorion enwogion*" long roll-along words, the meaning of which we hadn't a clue, but that didn't matter; we'd learnt them by the age of six, we were up there singing our hearts out, proving something about the Welsh education system, a sort of political declaration, had we known.

"*Da iawn! Da iawn!*" *Very good!* cried Mr Griffiths, and his friend Mr Pugh, another old pensioner, coughed and wheezed delightedly.

But we couldn't *speak* Welsh; we couldn't have a conversation. Nangi and Mr Griffiths had gone back to speaking between themselves, and presently Mr Pugh indicated over the counter, "Cigarettes, *os gwelwch yn dda*, Mrs Thomas," and Nangi had handed him a packet of Players, understanding what he had said. "*Diolch.*" *Thanks*. I gaped in awe.

I'd already vaguely sensed there were two worlds in Nangi's sweet shop, one for those who spoke Welsh and those who did not, Welsh-Welsh people and English-Welsh. Now that I was fourteen and taking the subject, I'd belong with Nangi and her customers. I'd be part of Nangi's secret Welsh life in Fforestfawr and, implicitly, of my father's, I thought hopefully.

***

"*Prynhawn da, merched!*" *Good afternoon, girls!*

We rose to our feet. "*Prynhawn da*, Miss Glynhower."

Thus signalled the beginning of *Dysgu Cymraeg*. *Learning Welsh*.

Miss Glynhower was sporting a chiffon scarf splattered with dragons, little green and red fiery creatures she invariably wore around the school, wafting over her shoulders in a delightful way. She had red hair that I now realised was dyed, given her age –

about forty-five – and bright red lipstick with matching red stiletto high heels that I imagined must be reprehensible to Miss Hodge in her stodgy, plain suit and clumpy heels. Miss Glynhower was romantic. Just the way she took charge of the eisteddfod each year on St David's Day in the old canteen told you that. She actually appeared on the stage swathed in the green robes of an arch-druid, with a crown of artificial oak leaves on her head. She'd wave a sword in a dangerous way over the heads of the *Gorsedd*, a specially chosen group of Welsh-speaking girls, also dressed as druids, who were to crown the school bards, the pinnacle of the eisteddfod. Miss Glynhower vehemently declared "*A oes heddwch?*" – *Is it peace?* – to which we all responded wildly, two hundred girls, "*Heddwch!*" – *Peace!* – more like a battle cry, Celts storming down the mountainsides led by our wild woman leader, Boadicea. This definitely alarmed Miss Hodge, who sat immobilised to the side of the hall since, as Miss Glynhower once confided, she did not "speak the tongue".

I straightened up in my seat and smiled at Miss Glynhower. I'd never been taught by an arch-druid before.

All the girls had crushes on Miss Glynhower. "I'm gonna name my first baby girl for 'er," vowed Beryl Edwards, and Patricia Jones said, "I already called my cat Olwen." I too was in love with Miss Glynhower.

Miss Glynhower was dynamic. First thing we had to learn right off was: "*Dw I'n dysgu cymraeg.*" *I am learning Welsh.* It was essential that any Welsh speaker you were planning to converse with know this, stressed Miss Glynhower. Welsh speakers *loved* to meet non-speakers learning the tongue. It was flattering. Secondly, to know how to comment on the weather was vital to getting a conversation going in Wales. "*Mae hi'n bwrw glaw,*" – *It is raining* – was guaranteed instant friendly response. We all tittered suitably.

The biggest mistake in conversing, warned Miss Glynhower, was to try to "translate" Welsh directly into English, which she called *Sais*. *Sais* was the "thin language" of the English. I was learning so much! For example: "our television" is said in Welsh:

"*ein teledu ni*" which, if translated literally, becomes "our television us"! You see how ridiculous that would sound to an Englishman.

"*Su'mae, Nangi,*" – Hello, Nangi – I said, a little shyly in the shop next Sunday. Drusilla rolled her eyes.

Nanny Thomas started behind the counter; she wasn't used to me calling her *Nangi* or speaking Welsh. But she smiled her little shy smile.

"Hi, Nanny," said Drusilla.

"*Sut wyt ti, Nangi? Dw I'n dysgu cymraeg yn ysgol. Mae bwrw glaw heddiw.*" *How are you, Nangi? I'm learning Welsh in school. It's raining today.* I was practising, ready for the old gents.

"I know," Nangi retorted shortly. She was shivering in her pinny, over which she'd stretched a cardigan. She had her Welsh Bible with a metal clasp with her, behind the counter. A small electric fire with three bars glowed near her feet. "The rain bin coming through them rafters all mornin'." A tin bucket stood on a table nearby to catch the flow.

I seemed to have exhausted the extent of my Welsh: hello, how are you, and the weather.

"Hello, Mam," breezed Father, following us in.

Nangi smiled. Her son. Cedric. He didn't say *Su'mae* to her. I'd never actually heard my father speak Welsh, something I'd not questioned until now. He wasn't Welsh-speaking, was not Welsh-Welsh then, I murmured, turning to him disappointed.

"'Ow the 'ell would I get a job, mun, without speaking English?" he cried. He was trying to tell me something.

He'd left school at fourteen, which meant he must have attended the awful board school in Mynydd Du (Black Hill), where he grew up. He showed it to us once, driving slowly by on the way home from Nangi's shop: his old school. I'd been terribly excited – a genuine old Welsh Board school likely going back to the Industrial Revolution.

"Tough, mun." Daddy had stared at the grim yard with its iron railings and riddled tarmac, a broken-down shed huddled in the corner for the toilet, which I now knew was called *ty bach*, "little house", though it looked more like a pigpen. "That's yewer 'eritage," Daddy had said drily. Drusilla didn't care, but Daddy was showing us something very terrible. That he'd left school at my age, fourteen, third form, looking for a job anywhere, in the oil works, the colliery, anything, not a career. (Miss Glynhower was vehement about the exploitation of the workers in industrial Wales. We were learning new vocabulary every day in Welsh class – oil, tin, steel, foundry, smelting, miner, pit, chains, explosion, disaster, death.)

"Lucky if you wuz still alive," said Nangi, and she opened the tureen of ice cream she had plugged in behind the counter. She had a long metal ladle she spooned out the ice cream with. "Choclit or vanilla?" she asked us.

"Chocolate, *os gwelwch yn dda*," I said, using Welsh for "please" proudly.

Drusilla rolled her eyes again. "When is this going to stop? I'll have the same, please, Nanny." Drusilla was determined to remain English-Welsh, speaking the Queen's English.

Presently two old gentlemen came in, shuffling and blowing, shaking the rain off their overcoats. "*Bore da*, Mrs Thomas. *Sut dych chi'n heddiw?*"

"*Go lew*, Mr Humphrey," said Nangi gloomily, pointing to the roof.

"*Duw duw!*" they echoed. *Duw – God!* – was an exclamation used all the time in Welsh.

"*Cwpaned o de,* Mr Humphrey?"

"Ah *diolch*, Mrs Thomas. *Gyda llaith, os gwelwch yn dda.*"

I thrilled. I'd actually understood everything being said in the secret language: that Nangi had offered Mr Humphrey a cup of tea – *cwpaned o de* – and he'd asked for it "with milk, please".

"Please" was another of those words Miss Glynhower had warned us against translating. "Please" in Welsh was four words long – "*os gwelwch yn dda*" – literally "if it pleases you good". "What a language!" Nanny Norman, our other grandmother would exclaim. She only spoke English, like most people in Swansea. As soon as the announcer on BBC Wales radio said, *"Dyma Rhaglen Cymry: Y Newyddion"* – *This is the Welsh Programme: The News* – she'd switch it off. "That rigmarole."

I'd been trying lately to rouse her interest in Welsh, letting her know what a beautiful captivating language she was missing. "You know, Nanny, there's about four ways to say 'yes' in Welsh. *Ie, oes, oedd…*" I said brightly.

Nanny Norman had stared. "Well, as long as you can say 'No!' to a boy, that's all that matters."

Perhaps, I thought, as I sat in Nangi's shop, that pointed to some mysterious difference between our two peoples.

The rain had turned misty outside, long grey smears spreading down the dirty glass windows. The shutters rattled, and rooks in the distant treetops outside shrieked and huddled together in the rookery near the parkey's house. Rain continued to plop from the rafters into the bucket.

Mr Humphrey and his pensioner friend of fifty years, Mr Pugh, were looking mournful, slowly stirring their teas at a table. It seemed old Mr Griffiths, who'd been one of Nangi's faithful, had passed away that very week, at ninety.

"Nawdeg!" exclaimed Nangi. *Ninety!* *"Mae'n ddrwg gen I."* *I'm sorry.*

She and Daddy bowed their heads a moment, along with Mr Humphrey and Mr Pugh. On the far wall was a lone poster – *PREPARE TO MEET THY DEATH* – and a smaller one, illustrated with a tankard of beer, and a finger pointing: *DEMON DRINK. The Temperance Society of Wales.*

"Delyd dy deynas, gwneler dy ewyllys," (*"Thy kingdom come, Thy will be done,"*) murmured Nangi, head still bowed. I recognised the words, which were from the Lord's Prayer in Welsh, recited at the Welsh service at school every Friday in the canteen (led by thrilling Miss Glynhower up on the stage). Nangi's eyes were squeezed tight as she prayed for Mr Griffiths' salvation. Nangi really meant it. Mr Humphrey and Mr Pugh did likewise. Drusilla pulled a mocking face as if to say "What next?"

Mr Pugh called out in English that Mr Griffiths was now "in 'eaven where Jesus was awaiting 'im, the old bugger," he added under his breath. Drusilla nudged me.

"Beautiful funeral at Capel Ebenezer, Mrs Thomas." Welsh-Welsh speaking people often broke into English in conversation whenever they felt like it. *Capel* was "chapel".

"Ah, *bendigedig!*" said Mr Pugh – *magnificent!* He was dressed in a three-piece suit that he wore for chapel, under his mackintosh. He had a high, silvery voice some Welsh men have; Daddy's was a deep baritone. Apparently Mr Pugh had worked in smelting with Mr Griffiths in their younger days. The smelting works. "Poor old dab," he said. Obviously one of Miss Glynhower's exploited. "*Swper neis ar Capel Ebenezer, wedyn, Mrs Thomas.*"

I thrilled again to understand that Mr Pugh was saying there'd been a nice supper afterwards at the chapel. *Neis – nice.* A lot of Welsh words sounded similar to English ones. Nangi must have missed Mr Griffiths' funeral because she couldn't take the day off work.

I wondered aloud why the chapel was called "Ebenezer", which reminded me of Scrooge's name in Dickens' *Christmas Carol.*

"*Duw*! Ebenezer means 'stone of help', Kezia," Mr Humphrey cried. "The Lord 'elped the prophet Samuel and the Israelites defeat their enemies, and Samuel lifted up a stone in commemorashun. *Samuel, One*, chapter seven, verses two to fourteen," he quoted. "Dun't yew know yewer Bible, Kezia? What for Skakespeare and no Bible?"

"They are 'Igh Church," said Nangi gloomily. "They dun' study the Bible like us Congregationals."

"I do know the Beatitudes and… Jesus raising Lazarus from the dead. And the fifteenth psalm," I said eagerly. Drusilla snorted and Daddy looked uncomfortable.

Mr Humphrey nodded and lifted his eyes toward the rafters. "*Lord, who shall abide in Thy tabernacle? Who shall dwell on Thy 'oly 'ill?*" he recited approvingly.

We understood that Nangi was a nonconformist Congregationalist, part of the *Anybunwyr*. She attended Ebenezer

Chapel on Maes Street, as did Mr Humphrey and Mr Pugh. The sweet shop was full of nonconformists! They did not approve of smoking, drink, undue sex (before marriage), lipstick, perfume, or high heels. They believed in something called Immersion Baptism, unlike the established Anglican Church whose priests subjected babies to what Nangi called disparagingly a "sprinkling" baptism, just a flick of water over the baby's head, she sniffed. I could now see, regretfully, how nonconformist baptism was far more thrilling and dramatic and genuine than our staid Anglican one. The Baptist communicant, dressed in white, crossed his hands over his chest and vowed "Jesus is my savior!" as the minister lowered him backwards into the pool, at the front of the chapel in front of the congregation, and submerged him totally under the surface while declaring him washed clean of his sins.

"Oh it's a fine sight," said Mr Humphrey. "A pure young boy, a lily bright, goin' under with the Lord's name on 'is lips."

Mr Pugh actually broke out into a hymn, "*Calon Lan*", which everyone sang at the rugby matches in Swansea. He had a high silvery treble.

"A clean heart overflowing with goodness,
Fairer than the lily bright…"
"*Calon lan yn llawn daioni,
Tecach yw na'r lili dlos…*"
He went on about "*canu'r dydd a chanu'r nos*" – *singing through the day and night* –

"*Da Iawn*, Mr Pugh!" cried Mr Humphrey, banging the table. "Very good! The tenor of Fforestfawr!"

Nangi grinned. She loved something impromptu; it brightened up the day. Rain was sloshing again through the rafters, filling the bucket.

Daddy was grinning too, enjoying it.

"This is crazy," muttered Drusilla. "They're all *twp*." One of the few Welsh words in her vocabulary she favoured, meaning daft in the head. "I'm not coming here anymore, I'm too old for this."

"Oh *dw I'n caru 'Canu'r dydd a chanu'r nos'*, Mr Pugh!" I cried, eager to be part of it. I'd said in Welsh: "*I also love 'singing day and night'.*"

"Well, now, *diolch, Kezia. Siaradwch chi'n Cymraeg, fachgen*?" Mr Pugh was asking me if I spoke Welsh, calling me *fachgen*, an endearment that meant "little one". I thrilled.

"What 'appen to 'er German?" said Nangi dolefully.

Daddy shrugged. "I dunno what's got in 'er 'ead lately, with all this Welsh."

For the first time I sensed their disappointment in me. Daddy and Nangi had delighted in poring over my school reports over the years. "Tops again in English!" Nangi would cry, and pass the report card over the counter to Mr Griffiths (before he passed) and Mr Humphrey, who'd say "There's brainy then." But now my 90% in Welsh drew little praise from Nangi; her adulation was for English and Shakespeare. Nangi once bought me *Lamb's Tales from Shakespeare* for my seventh birthday. I wondered now how Nangi had known of that lovely book of literature when she could barely read or write, in English anyway. She'd left school at ten ("no money for books an' shoes"). Had a kindly bookseller advised her, a little Welsh-speaking woman dressed in black asking for a fine book for her brainy granddaughter? I winced now at the thought of all the pennies she must have saved for such a fine gift. "I wunts 'er to read Shakespeare!" And where, pray, had she learned of Shakespeare, in the narrow gritty row housing in Mynydd Du, Black Mountain, where she'd been born and raised? She'd lived all her life between Davies Row and Middle Road, the extent of one street, flaring smoke stacks from the colliery at the bottom of the hill. She likely never played again after age ten. Now that I was fourteen and understanding Welsh, I interpreted it better. I understood something. That Nangi longed for me to excel in my studies, excel in Shakespeare! She and Daddy didn't seem to appreciate how wonderful Miss Glynhower was teaching us the ancient heritage of our Welsh heroes Prince Llewelyn and Madoc ap Owain ap Gruffydd and Owain Glyndwr, (the *real* Prince of

Wales, according to Miss Glynhower, who knew). It seemed the descendant of Owain Glyndwr was living right then in Soho, working as a waiter, awaiting his moment to return to Wales and lead the Welsh people like Nangi and Mr Pugh and Mr Humphrey to regain their rightful kingdom, which seemed to include England. Miss Glynhower's idea was to actually overthrow the Crown, I murmured.

"Like 'ell she will," said Daddy.

But Mr Humphrey was getting excited. "*Bendigedig*, Kezia! *Mae Owain Glyndwr Tywysog o Gymru*!" – *Owain Glyndwr is Prince of Wales!* The word *Tywysog*, "prince", had a fine flair to it, I thought.

Nangi was more concerned about the rain coming again through the rafters, filling a second bucket.

"Better call Mr Greene, Mam. It's 'is job to fix it, he's the owner, mun," said Daddy.

So Nangi did not own the sweet shop of Ravencliff Park after all, as Drusilla and I had believed all these years as children, but a Mr Greene did, Nangi's boss. She served ice cream and sweets and tea and cakes all day long, put up the shutters by herself at closing time and walked home through the park in the dusk in her hobnailed boots, alone, unafraid of the cosh boys who sometimes broke into the shop.

"I takes them thugs, them cosh boys to court before the magistrate, and they gets sent to borstal," she cried vehemently. "I dun' stand no nonsense!"

"*Duw!* Right yew are, Mrs Thomas," cried the old gents, pulling on their mackintoshes.

"You better be careful, Mam, all the same, they might come after you," warned Dad.

Cosh boys were mean; they dressed fancy in long-sleeved coats and had greased hair and thick, crepe rubber wedged shoes called "creepers". They carried razors.

"Slash yewer face in soon as look at ew, Mrs Thomas," agreed Mr Pugh. Carve Nangi up.

"Tut, tut!" went the old gents, concerned, straightening their overcoats.

"Well, *Ffarwel,* Mrs Thomas. See you next Sunday."

"*Hwyl.*" Goodbye.

Mr Humphrey and Mr Pugh went out to brave the tempest.

I felt sorry to leave. Sorry for Nangi facing the rest of the day in a shop with a leaking roof. I looked at it with older eyes now. The sweet shop was a small place, a narrow rectangle with two big windows overlooking the park that she boarded up when she left. Some tables and metal chairs here and there, and a long wooden bench which stood against the wall, and the grim counter with a chair behind it for Nangi to sit on with her Bible. A dreary place on a long rainy Sunday with no customers coming by, I reflected for the first time, now that I was fourteen and speaking Welsh. For until then I'd only been interested in enjoying an ice cream cone with Drusilla.

Ffarwel, Nangi, farewell. I turned away reluctantly… *Ffarwel,* my fierce little nonconformist grandmother. "*Hwyl!*"

MISS HODGE

"Isn't that Mr Thomas, yewer father over there, Kezia?"

Of course I'd seen him as soon as I'd walked through the gates. It was four o'clock, home time, and there was my father astride his idling motorbike, beaming proudly in that awful way with his stained teeth. He gave a little wave. He loved seeing me in my grammar school uniform; I was the first in his family to pass scholarship and go to the girls' county grammar school. He was on his way home from work, another source of shame.

"Oh, so it is!" I cried brightly, tossing my curls.

I waved back. Of course it didn't take in anyone, least of all Enid and Gaynor, who watched covertly from under their berets, taking in Father's oily togs and his canvas haversack and billycan slung over his shoulder. He did shift work at Tir John power station, so needed to take some food to work. Gay's father was a store manager and drove a car, a Vauxhall Velox. Enid's father, Mr Griffiths, worked in the tin plate foundry. I'd met him once in Enid's back kitchen in the council house the Griffiths lived in on Penlas estate. He'd looked insane standing by the sink in his vest, his hair sticking up like chicken feathers and his thin, sensitive face, too sensitive for a man, tightening. Yes, the face of a man who could not face the world as a tin plate worker when he was so brilliant. Enid had confided this to me and you believed it. Mr Griffiths was well-read: he took *The Times Literary Supplement* and *The Guardian*. He didn't own as much as a bicycle, but at least he never turned up at the school gates looking mental. My father didn't look mental or sensitive. His rough red face spoke of wind velocity on a motorbike at eighty mph.

"Hi Dad!" I crossed the road.

"'Lo, Kezia. Hop on the back, and mind yewer curls."

He had on huge leather gloves like a mammoth's in size. I only hoped Miss Grayson who taught English literature wasn't walking out through the gates. She lived in *Cartref* on classy Sketty Road.

I had to shift my satchel onto my back like a tortoise shell and, worse, part my legs astride the pillion. My tunic pulled up above my knees, while Gay and Enid and batches of interested girls watched from the opposite kerb.

Father kicked up the bike in the most horrible way, and with a deafening roar we took off, the sound terrifying old ladies sitting out in their glass porches for the afternoon sun, which Father was oblivious to. I placed one finger gingerly on his back for balance, hating to be this close to him, and we shot forward at fifty mph down Glynmor Road, leaving balls of exhaust, surely against the law.

"There goes Kezia Thomas on her father's motor-bike."

My tie wrapped itself round my neck. I had to hold on to my beret, of course, otherwise it would go flying down Glynmor Road and my father would have to stop the bike. Bits of hair slapped my cheeks, my eyes keening against the wind. Soon we were out on the Mumbles road, far from the grammar school and the tidy middle-class houses with their laurel hedges and porches and clean, clipped lawns. The road went round the bay. Suddenly there was the sea, wild and rolling. The tide was in; glorious, threshing, tempestuous waves behind a row of dark pines, wild greyish sea on the rise. Gulls swooped and wheeled; there was the whiff of ozone, salty and sweet as we roared by.

"Lovely, aye?" yelled Father backwards in the wind.

In the bedroom upstairs I took off my uniform and hung it in the cupboard I had to share with my twin sister. She'd be home later. I wondered how Drusilla always managed to evade Father after school. Did she take the upper gate and go along Brynmawr Road and catch the bus there? I put on my old skirt and top, and wool slippers. Then I went back downstairs to lay the fire. You had to roll balls of newspaper and put them down first in the grate, then thin sticks of kindling, and on top of that lumps of anthracite from the coal shed. Father would add small coals later to bank it down, but as I lit a match everything flared lovely and bright from the anthracite. I loved it when Mammy came home tired from work and said, "Ooh there's a lovely fire!" Father was getting out the spuds to peel for chips, so I got on with the ironing and rolling the socks into balls.

***

I'd won a blue ribbon for art in the eisteddfod, lower school, first prize, beating out even Enid, in the self-portrait class.

"You look *twp*, cross-eyed," Drusilla said. "What d'you do that to your face for? Miss Tedwyn must be cross-eyed too, to give you a prize for that."

"Psychologically outstanding," Miss Tedwyn had said as I'd gone up on the stage for my ribbon. And everyone had laughed at my nom-de-plume, "Bubbles", which I'd chosen to throw off the judges. Every contestant had had to use a nom-de-plume so there would be no favouritism. Enid had chosen "Finlandia", very austere and beautiful; no one laughed at that. She won in every class with her beautiful landscapes.

So "Bubbles" I became, the popular madcap of the third form I was trying to be: Kezia Thomas with the cute kiss curls who at the same time flummoxed the staff. I'd cut my hair short and curled it, the frowning serious girl in the portrait forgotten. But then I had to keep up being bubbly. It meant putting my hair in clips every night to go to bed. The metal pressed into my scalp all night long like little daggers whichever way I turned, but it was worth it. Of course, sometimes I got tired of wetting my hair with spit and twisting it into the clips after cleaning my teeth. I looked enviously at Drusilla's naturally wavy hair framing her face; she never had to do anything. But then, I thought, what would happen to me, who would I be now without "Bubbles"? And I put in the hard, hurtful clips again, to change my straight hair.

Of course, this put me at Drusilla's mercy. She could say at any time she liked, at the bus stop or, worse, in front of the prefects, that my curls weren't real, I put my hair in clips every night. So I was careful to avoid Drusilla at school, and going to and fro as well. It was a bit of a bind. I had to take the later bus in the morning which meant the trudge up Glynmor Hill not to be late for the bell, my satchel bumping on my back and my chest hurting. It was easy to avoid her in school as she was in D form, cookery and sewing, while I was in form A, the Latin class. All of which was captivating.

So now if Father were to pick me up, it would be all be part of being Bubbles, the irrepressible madcap – "There goes Bubbles!"

Bubbles – madcap, but artistic with it – "She won a first, you know, in the eisteddfod." Every so often I got all my books together in a corner of the living room, blocking out the drone of the television, and studied hard, memorising my Latin verbs over and over before going upstairs to put in my clips. It wouldn't do for Bubbles to be a duffer; the secret was to be smart with it, too – tops in English and Latin every term "and she never even swots" was Bubbles' reputation.

"It's not fair!" went pretty Eirlys Evans enviously. She studied Latin conjunctives like mad for every test, doing her homework solidly, painstakingly, and never got an A.

***

I pirouetted into the senior library, tossing my tunic pleats and my head of curls. The prefects were swotting Latin, Horace and Catullus, set pieces for translation in the sixth form, at the long oak table. There was that hush that comes from volumes of books on musty shelves that had been there since the war.

"Kezia Thomas announcing her arrival," drawled Miss Bentham in her sarcastic way. She was from Twickenham, hence "Twicky" round the school. She taught Tudors and Stuarts. "Making sure she's the centre of attention wherever she goes," she went on relentlessly in her cutting way I always enjoyed when it was at other girls' expense, rocking with mirth – *"No, Moira, Elizabeth the First was not queen for forty years because she was a virgin."*

The prefects nudged each other; Kezia Thomas was getting it from Twicky, so of course I had to toss my head defiantly to show Bubbles could not be pricked.

"Watch me." I winked at Enid.

With a little moan I fell to the floor with a slump. I fluttered my eyes. I could hear some prefect shout, and Enid's gasp: "Kezia Thomas has passed out, Miss Bentham." I tried to look passed out, keeping very still.

More cries and exclamations – this was a real lark – then the clump of Twicky's brogues and an exasperated "Oh!" I looked up, affecting confusion, holding my hot face, not sure whether fainted girls were not dead pale.

"You can come out of your little fit," said Twicky drily, "and find your way to the headmistress's office. Next time you faint, remember to stay supine for at least ten minutes."

***

"The whole school's talking about your fainting fit, you're in for it," said Drusilla. "You're not right in the head, they've had enough of you."

Drusilla put down the jam sponge pudding she'd made in cookery that day. She was the sister of Bubbles who might get gated, and was becoming famous. I was confident Mother would get me out of this. She'd been called up the school to see Miss Hodge, the headmistress. Miss Hodge would see how gracious and tall Mother was, with her patrician nose and fine bones and natural curls. Mother would wear the smart grey suit she wore to the office where she was head secretary to Professor Bowling at the university. Miss Hodge would be impressed. Mother was beautifully spoken.

"You're not gonna get out of this," crowed Drusilla.

I spent the next day at home, suspended from school. I stared out of the window, alone in the house, which was strange and cold. Rain slanted down the pane, the houses opposite grey in the mist. I shivered in my shirt as there was no fire. Mother would go straight to the office after the interview with Miss Hodge, Father was at work – he was on morning shift that week, and Drusilla was in school. My uniform hung in the cupboard like an empty person, another girl's skin: the serge tunic, striped school tie, stiff white shirt. I shut the door quickly.

"Now then," Mother said sharply after she got in. "I had a long talk with Miss Hodge this morning. And you can take that smirk off your face, Kezia. There'll be no more of *this* nonsense, for a start." Mother took my clips and threw them in the bin. You could hear tiny splintering sounds. Oh, Bubbles!

Mother towered over me:

"From now on you'll do your hair as I say. You're going to be expelled, get it? Yes, thrown out of school. So get down on your hands and knees, my girl, and start cleaning the grate."

I went at once into the living room and got down on my knees and starting sweeping out the cinders. Presently I heard Father in the kitchen whispering, "Dun't yew think yew're being a bit hard on 'er?"

Mutterings from Mother as she banged some pans, then: "She's got to learn a lesson, scare her a bit."

I began to sweep the cinders onto a sheet of newspaper. Mother had obviously colluded with Miss Hodge in an unpleasant way. I wasn't a daughter to be proud of, to be excused. And never again to wear the grammar school uniform I knew I couldn't now exist without, or have curls. There was the possibility I'd go to the board school and wear ordinary clothes, and not carry a satchel for the neighbours to see I was a grammar school girl. Mother couldn't mean it. I didn't dare put the light on in the living room; best to stay on my knees riddling ashes in the dark, out of the way.

Presently a length of light broke under the door and Father tiptoed in. He put a finger to his lips, looking sorrowful, then knelt down beside me. There was a whiff of grease and heavy male sweat.

"It's OK, Kezia, dun't cry," he whispered. "You're not really gonna be expelled, but dun't let on to yewer mother I told you. Just do what she says for now." He patted my head before tiptoeing out.

I felt a rush of relief, and hope. I might wear my uniform again. I finished the cinders, laid out the balls of newspaper and kindling for the fire. Of course, Miss Hodge must have been impressed with Mother.

Next morning, Father said to get on my uniform, we was going up the school. No kid of his was going to be denied an educashun.

But –

"But Dad, I'm gated. We have to wait for notification from Miss Hodge."

If only Mother were here, but she always left early for work.

"Notificashun nuthin'. You're going back to class."

"But Dad, we can't just walk in, unannounced."

I meant Father in his togs. In goggles, standing before Miss Hodge. The office, with its brass plate outside – *miss Hilda Hodge, Headmistress* – was a terrifying place, large oak desk in the window, mounds of documents on top stamped Glynmor Girls' County Grammar School, behind which Miss Hodge sat in a tweed suit. Father just did not understand that a summons to Miss Hodge was like a call before a military tribunal.

"Dun't worry, she's expecting us."

Father, who didn't know what an *h* was, had obviously called Miss Hodge, whom he must have addressed as "Miss 'Odge". He must have walked up the road to the telephone box at the top of the hill and called the school from there. I felt a tight pain akin to panic: Miss 'Ilda 'Odge, the 'eadmistress.

"I don't mind staying home, Dad, honest."

"Get yewer beret on."

With its gold and green crest.

The private homes on Glynmor Road gleamed quietly in the sun as Father drew up to the school. He parked at the roadside, resting his bike on the kerb. All the girls were in class; it was very quiet, just a few birds fluttering round the deserted yard and the canteen.

"Go get Miss 'Odge."

"Oh, but Dad, we have to go to her office." Gay and Enid and Beryl Oskins, especially, would observe through the glass partitions my father and me crossing the quad in the middle of French. We would have to negotiate the netball pitch up to Miss Hodge's domain. "She won't come down here, Dad."

It was blowing a wet wind.

Father didn't understand you just didn't summons the headmistress to the edge of a road.

"She'll come. You'll see."

He was still astride his motorbike, balancing it with one foot. He wore black oilskins sweating like animal skins, black leather gloves up to his elbows, and those awful plastic goggles pushed up on his forehead.

Slowly I headed across the quadrangle, hoping Miss Hodge was out attending a board meeting, but she was at her desk. I could see her outline through the window that overlooked quad and classrooms. The brass plate shone on the wall outside: *headmistress*.

I tapped on the door.

Miss Hodge opened it with a frown. "Yes?"

"Please, Miss Hodge, my father's here to see you. I'm sorry, he says he can't come up, he's down on the road, he's on his way to work," I added lamely.

Miss Hodge hesitated, and sighed. She turned to her secretary, Miss Bryce, who sat at the back of the room at a small table, taking dictation. "I'll be back shortly, Frances. It's Mr Thomas."

Without another word, Miss Hodge walked out across the netball pitch, her hips swaying. She had tiny feet in heeled black shoes that stumbled over the asphalt. You could hear the hum of girls' voices drifting up in unison from the south verandah. "*Je parle, tu parle, il…*"

I walked in silence beside her, confused. What must my father have said to Miss Hodge on the phone to bring things to this?

He was standing by the kerb next to his bike. Unmistakably a working man, no messing with him, just as Miss Hodge, with her solid tweeds and permanently waved hair, was headmistress.

At the beginning of the year I'd put down "engineer" as my father's occupation on the school form. I hung my head, with its new straight hair clinging round my neck. Oh this was the death of Bubbles, of everything.

There was the school canteen, a piece of asphalt, wrought iron railings and the road. It was a delicate moment as to where exactly Miss Hodge would stand. Would she shout to Father over the wrought iron railings, or stand next to him at the kerb, outside school boundaries? I closed my eyes. Miss Hodge hesitated, confused. Father held his ground, his tiny eyes scrunched behind his round wire National Health glasses. Miss Hodge braced herself, and manoeuvred her solid legs almost at the railings, crossing the line somewhat on the grass verge. The encounter was to take place on Father's territory.

"You Miss 'Odge, the 'eadmistress?" Father did not extend his hand. "Cedric Thomas here, Kezia's father."

"I am Miss Hodge, Mr Thomas, and—"

"Now look 'ere, Miss 'Odge, I 'aven't got all day, I'm a working man."

Miss Hodge flinched.

"I wunts my daughter back in school where she belongs. If yew are 'aving trouble with 'er at school, that's yewer problem not mine, but she's entitled to an educashun."

Miss Hodge made as if to speak; her mouth opened and closed.

"I dun't tell yew what to do with 'er inside yewer walls, that's for yew to decide. But she's a good girl at 'ome to 'er mother. Irons all the clothes, cleans out the grate, scrubs the kitchen floor," went Father relentlessly.

I could never be Bubbles again, of course. The cute, irresponsible, bubbly third-former of the girls' county grammar school had expired.

Father looked defiantly up at Miss Hodge, who remained impassive. "Well, I gotta be on the turbines at one."

Miss Hodge looked vaguely in pain.

With that, Father jumped on his bike, gave the starter a good kick and revved it up. The accelerator seemed to explode in Miss Hodge's face, and he was gone in a ball of exhaust and smoke down Glynmor Road, my mighty knight in oilskins, with the ear flaps over his ears.

Miss Hodge spun on her heels. Father had won, I saw that. I followed heavily, head down, doomed forever to be the good girl he saw I was: kind, loyal, loving, a good little scrubber; not knowing how extraordinary that was.

WASHING THE GRAVES

"Can't bury someone in the normal fashion. Got to be different!" (Or secretive, I wonder now.) "All this melodrama!" My mother snorted, straightening her worn hat in the cracked mirror over the sink.

"'S not melodrama, Mavis, mun," my father insisted, red-faced and unhappy. It was his nephew, our cousin Derek who had died. I didn't know how, didn't wonder then. "They just don't want people *seeing* that's all."

His face was red and flustered from – he swore in a hiss at my unperturbed mother – the white starched collar she'd insisted he wore, half choking him to death. He could have stepped out of it and it would have stood up on its own, the starch she'd put in it.

The electric light glowed strange and pale as though it were midnight in the small, stone-floored kitchen. The bread had tasted sour, the milk a bit off. Mammy pulled on my woolly hat and got out mittens for the cold. I was still sick with measles. Drusilla was being minded at Nanny's house in town by Nanny Norman.

The front door slammed. We clattered noisily yet in silence down the front path to the gate. Night lamps were still burning in the streets. A heavy salt wind blew in great draughts up Mount Pleasant hill from the sea through the sleeping town below, like a flue funnelling up the icy streets. The boats anchored at bay huddled together, their star lights winking. A sudden violet flare gushed across the water from the steelworks at Margham – the Steel Company of Wales, I thought proudly.

"Look! Daddy!" I cried.

We'd reached the church. It was Catholic, called St Mary's, standing at the top of the hill, near the roundabout. The land sloped away on one side, dropping into heather and common. The church had a cross on the roof and stained glass windows of saints and holy painted gilt images that our Nanny Thomas, a Welsh Nonconformist, disapproved of, regarding such things as popery. She had once sworn never to set foot inside any Papist place, let her be struck down dead on the spot, but she was there, waiting in the porch with old Aunty Beat, dressed in her old black squirrel coat of many years and black felt hat to match, with its low brim from which the cheap Marks and Spencer's diamante lizard had carefully been removed. A fresh oblong space could distinctly be seen where it had clung for many years.

"Hush, Kezia. You're not supposed ter be with us," said Mammy.

"'Taint right for childrun to see the dead. Especially girls," Nangi sniffed. "It can 'ave effects on them. They grows up crooked."

"Right yew are!" poor old Aunty Beat trembled. She had the palsy, Mother always whispered whenever she saw her, which was usually at a funeral.

"But she's recovering from measles," my mother cried, rather loudly. "We just can't leave her alone in the house."

There was a brief reassessment: after all, they agreed bitterly, perhaps the three generations should be represented. That was only right. Kezia should be witness.

Everyone was there: Miss Enid Rhys, the dead one's teacher; and Dilys and Gwilfer, my Welsh-speaking second cousins; Uncle Terence and Aunt Elizabeth from Devon. And of course, Aunty Lili-Mai, the dead one's mother. Her husband, Uncle Kevin, was the Catholic. He stood up front, in the pew nearest the coffin, next to Aunty Lili-Mai. Tears trickled down his face and his neck, and a stiff white collar like Daddy's. He seemed to be heaving, and his thin blue eyes cocked sideways, as though he were squinting.

He was tough. (He worked on the docks, I'd heard said.) He had a short body, broad shoulders, and a square head. He was wearing a dark blue suit that pulled across his shoulders because of his muscles. Usually he was a jolly man.

Aunty Lili-Mai stood very erect, frowning, severe. She never cried. She looked dull and ugly – "Utterly washed out," said Mammy. "She may as well lie down dead in that coffin with him."

"Hush, Mavis," said Daddy.

Afterwards, everyone congregated for a few last moments on the paving outside. It was still dark, because autumn had come and the clocks gone back, said someone. The town still glittered below in a myriad of night lights, but it was clearer, sharper. The world was more distinct, for during the vigil the sun had swung slowly over the pier, and a pale, yellowy, ghostly gleam passed over the boats and stirring water. "O wondrous light!" the priest had intoned, swinging the censer and walking round the coffin. Derek it seemed had passed beyond into that light that hovered, the Father had assured, high above the stars that were scattered still in a million shreds overhead. In his going there had been ten wax candles, and boys in flowing white robes with frills who tended silently the putting out of the flames in the wicks. They had genuflected low to the images of Jesus and his mother called Mary, whose robe was painted blue. Her eyes looked down. There had been six pallbearers all in black. The lid of the coffin clamped to with a reverberating bang: Derek Rhys Macnamara, age seventeen. That was death.

Everyone began shuffling to the outer gates with their spiked wrought-iron railings. Old Nangi was bent quietly over the path, very pale, like wax. She neither spoke nor cried, despite the few secret tears trickling down the powder. One tight blue curl, which had been pressed in clips all night, turned to fuzz in the damp wind.

Nangi clutched her shiny black patent leather bag. Tomorrow she would be back at the shop in Ravencliff Park, serving sweets and ice cream and cigarettes. She snapped her lips tight: grief was too deep a thing for mere floods of tears, too secret and terrible; for to show the grief that was terrible as wrath was humiliation. It must be suffered in secret, obdurate to the end.

"Why don't they all have a good cry and get it over with once and for all, like normal people?" hissed my mother angrily, with a swollen red face. She took me home, but not before I saw a sudden gust blow them, like a flock of black birds, against the gates.

Everyone stepped out and walked through the cold streets to the cemetery. The only distinction the burial claimed was that it was the last time women were allowed to attend interment in Wales.

"Lucky fer us," Nangi said gloomily. "We wuz the last."

**

Life resumed. Our father trundled back to the power station at Tir John, to turn the turbines for the town's electricity. Aunty Lili-Mai and Uncle Kevin remained in the little red-brick council house overlooking hills near Pantygwydr Road. They even had a new little son, a new cousin for Drusilla and me, in a year, Mansel Macnamara. We forgot Derek. We hung around Aunty Lili-Mae's kitchen, hoping she'd pull out her breast from her open blouse and feed the baby, see her big pink teat, but Daddy spoiled it. He'd say, "Come outa there into the front room, you two."

Dilys, who lived in one of the miners' cottages with her mother, our Great Aunty Beat, and her brother Gwilfer, returned to her vegetable plot, and Gwilfer to his birds at the bottom of the garden. The birdhouse reeked with a warm, pungent, sweet smell of moist feathers and poop. Up the hill in her little shop, Nanny Thomas put on her criss-cross flowery pinny, nailed up the wooden shutters by herself ready for winter's worst, and filled in the month's orders for the sweets, tobacco and chocolates for Mr Greene. She made a whole tureen of vanilla ice cream and scrubbed the floors. There were bats up in the rafters, hanging upside down. "They comes out at dusk. Wunt an ice cream?"

"Yes please, Nanny."

Rooks were gathered in the tall treetops, making a terrible din as we walked back down through the park to Aunty Beat's place at the crossroad.

Great Aunty Beat stood stirring a tub of washing in the lean-to. She was dressed in a faded print and a pinny, and heelless slippers. We'd come under the archway at the side of the cottages, which were below street level, though Drusilla and I didn't realise that then. It meant the bedroom window facing the road was below the level of the pavement. Later on, in grammar school I learned that an old road on a lower level had run there in the nineteenth century, the miners' cottages belonging to another era, something we only sensed. The old sooty stones of the archway were low over our heads, and when we came out on the other side, pretty weeds of yellow flowers thrust up between the cobblestones and layers of moss. We came shyly out into a blaze of light. We were in the back gardens shared by all the tenants of the cottages. There were flowers and sagging trellises of sweet peas in profusion that they had planted. A big tap was shared by all for water and that too had pretty weeds curling round the base. We sidled forward, holding hands, to the doorway of the lean-to, dressed in our fresh white, homemade, starched frocks and shining ribbons, our ringlets hanging in a row.

"Aw, Mam, ain't they *lovely*!" sighed Dilys, looking up, her big broad face breaking into a smile. She was peeling taters in a tub of cold water and she too had raw red hands. She'd wound a scarf round her head, tied in a twist in front like butterfly wings. She wore dark overalls.

"Aah, Georgie's little girls! *The twins*!" trembled Aunty Beat. She said this every Sunday when we visited. She stopped stirring the washing in the sink and gave us a big smile, coming towards us with open arms; she loved us so much. She couldn't stop trembling. It was something called "dropsy", Mammy said. Her hands trembled and shook awful; you tried not to look. "Poor old dabs," our other nanny, Nanny Norman, would say, meaning they were poor, poorer than Nanny Norman, who was not poor at all but lived in a tall old house in town and went to Austria with a seniors' group for her summer vacation. So we understood that Daddy's relatives – his side of the family, but ours too – were not on the same footing, but though we didn't really understand, we knew to care.

There was a tin bath hanging on a hook inside the wash house. To have a bath, Aunty Beat boiled tons of water in the cauldrons over the fire and filled the tin bath, which was brought in and set in front of the hearth, nice and cosy. You sat in the hot water up to your chest, said Gwilfer, and splashed yourself, and looked at the fire. I thought of our superior bathroom upstairs in our council house, but icy cold and lonely. I wondered in awe if they pulled the lace curtain at the parlour window while they bathed naked so no one could see in (there was something exciting about this). Mammy asked once, didn't they all use the same water? There was a hint of something in her voice, and Daddy retorted, "Well didn't we all during the war, mun?"

Drusilla and I sat on the Welsh settle, side by side under the small paned window, loving it. There was just the one tiny room they all lived in, crammed with furniture. Another room down a passage hidden behind a thick curtain was mysteriously shut up. It was the "best room", Aunty Beat would say, with deference. No one went in there; it was only for the minister of Ebenezer Chapel or dead relatives who'd passed, lying in their coffins before they were buried.

Once Nanny Thomas came from work for her tea. She'd locked up the sweet shop and let down the shutters early and walked down to the Cross by herself and come under the tunnel. She'd come so that after supper she could go to evening chapel with Aunty Beat and Dilys. The chapel was a small, homely white-washed building on Maes Street; Nonconformist Congregationalist, and the service was in Welsh.

Nanny Thomas had sat in the corner armchair by the fire. The kettle was singing over the coals.

"Warm yewer self, Lil," said Aunty Beat, pouring Nangi a cup of tea.

"Thank yew, Beatrice," said Nangi. (So "Beat" was short for "Beatrice", and we'd never known.)

We stayed sitting round-eyed on the settle, taking our nangi in, realising she was tiny, even though she was Aunty Beat's sister. We'd only seen Nangi behind the counter in her shop; we'd never known how tall or short she was.

The settle was hard, of black oak; the window had small square panes and the sill was so sweet with pots of herbs on it for the sun. More herbs hung in bunches from hooks in the rafters, drying out. Was that what made it like the nineteenth century, when these were miners' cottages? It was a question I pondered much later in my teens, at the girls' grammar school.

"Yewer granpa wuz a miner," Aunty Beat's voice had quivered, another time, in pride. Like her dead husband Dai. We understood we were to be proud of that, miners' grandchildren. We nodded our heads of curls in agreement. "But he be long gone."

The fire crackled and spit in the grate. A cauldron hung down from a big nail above, simmering meat and vegetables, 'tatoes and swede from the garden. The teapot was left to steep on the hob. An aroma of fresh bread and hot pastry arose from inside the wall bricks by the fire. Aunty Beat took a long, curved iron poker and pulled open a door beside the fireplace. Inside was a hot little oven filled with loaves of bread.

"Oh-h!" we breathed. It was a secret. Aunty Beat didn't have an oven like Nanny Norman's.

Aunty Beat shook with excitement and drew out an apple pie with the hook. It was hot and juicy. "There we are!" I felt sad as she shook and trembled cutting us each a slice.

"Mind yew dun' burn yewer tongues," said Dilys, who was standing by watching from the doorway. She still had on her canvas overalls, and the sleeves of her blouse were rolled up above the elbows, giving her a tough look. How old was she? We did not know and dared not ask.

We stayed on the settle, side by side, eating pie in our laps, then Drusilla began playing with the kittens. "Oh I'd love one."

"No use of cats," said Daddy. He stood in the doorway, his presence filling the room. He frowned at the sound of hymns playing on a radio that ran on batteries. The radio was on top of the bureau. "Dun' know why they plays 'ymns," he muttered.

"Lord, Redeemer of my soul." Suddenly it changed to Welsh, *"O Iesu mawr,"* which meant O great Jesus.

"Aah, Georgie!" smiled Aunty Beat fondly. She always called Daddy by his baby name instead of Cedric. I pondered that, that she loved his baby name. Daddy had been called by his middle name, George. Perhaps Nangi used to take him to the cottage in a wooden pram for Dilys and Gwilfer to play with him as children.

No mention of Derek. We too had forgotten him, our distant dead cousin. There was just the brownish faded old photo of him leaning next to the Toby jug on the dresser, snapped one summer down Crawley Woods. "Derek" was faintly scratched underneath, and "1944", the year before he died at the end of the war. He was wearing plus-fours and a checked shirt, and was pressing the bell of his bicycle. But nobody spoke of him.

***

The redcurrants burst into a fiery blaze. Drusilla and I had wandered down the bright, cool garden. It was late summertime. Jasmine, honeysuckle, amaryllis and dog-daisies rose in profusion round the old birdhouse.

Gradually, secretly, like a last blossom in deep dark woods, the Dead One shimmered in our consciousness. In the resplendent September sunlight that caught the little window panes on the backs of the cottages in little flames, the world shone. The hills beyond the bottom hedge lit up, the river glittered between the chapels. Apples swelled and grew rosy, and so heavy their boughs hung eventually to the ground. The strange silence of a late summer day hovered, the mist rising from the valley, a pale sweet shroud.

Gwilfer was standing framed in the doorway of the birdhouse, just home from shift.

"Gwilfer!" I cried. "The Dead One, our cousin, is not dead, is he? '*Lo I am with you always, even unto the end of the world.*'" I recited a text from Sunday School.

"The Bible says! The Bible says!" he quivered. "The Bible says a lot of bloody things."

The birdhouse was small, enclosed and hot, like a box. It stank with the strange sweet-sour odour of birds and nesting boxes and sweet damp hay for them to lay their eggs in. There was a tiny, hot skylight in the roof. The birds, little canaries, fluttered and squeaked in their cages.

"See!" Gwilfer lifted up a new little nestling for Drusilla to see closer. Drusilla was the prettiest one. Gwilfer was like a bird himself, with his glistening hooked nose and glittering little eyes. His hair stuck up in thin sprouts, like feathers. "Poor little bugger," he said. "Won't last long, mother hen wont feed 'im."

"Oh-h!" We were shocked.

"Too weak, mun."

"But shouldn't she try all the more, then?" I persisted, trying not to cry.

"Nah! She feeds the one what 'as the best chance to survive."

"Ah!" said Drusilla. "So fluffy!"

"Well. That's life – and death."

Gwilfer worked on the railways, cleaning the tracks down the tunnels, kneeling and digging out dirt and rubbish so the trains went over the rails smoothly. He'd recently come across his mate run over by a train in the dark, he said. It come so fast, roaring down the tunnel. Gwilfer had found him all mashed up without no face left, he said. We thrilled. "Didn' 'ear it coming, poor devil."

Of course this was not for Mammy and Nanny Norman to know. We understood not to tell, not to betray Gwilfer; we sensed being a railway worker was not the best sort of job, when you came across best friends mashed to death by a train. Mammy would give that knowing look and purse her lips concerning these relatives, though she never openly said anything against them.

***

I remember the moment I changed forever, inside. It was in the girls' grammar school, and I was a senior girl in sixth form. Drusilla had left school a year earlier and gone to Gregg's commercial college to learn shorthand and typing. She already had a job in an office, earning her own money, and had a boyfriend, which meant she was grown-up at seventeen. Soon I'd be leaving school too, forever. Going on to university – the first in the family, beamed Daddy. Nanny Thomas glowed in her shop, 'er gran'daughter going to the university. The world opened wide and mysterious – what was going to happen? I didn't think about boys or getting married. I was to study. I was to find out everything through books.

It was morning milk break in the classroom. A small coterie of girls was clustered by the rads to get warm. Room 10 was always freezing; the pipes gone bust again. Hettie and I sat on the desks sucking milk up through our straws from the half-pint milk bottles we got each morning at break. Hettie's long legs stuck out from under her skirt; you were allowed to wear skirts as seniors, no more of those horrid shapeless tunics. I could make out Maira Glynn's low voice carrying across the room from the radiator, saying, "… and they have *no* electricity or hot running water, they bathes *in the same old tin bath* in front of the fire, honest! And do their washing in a lean-to, scrubbing *by hand*!"

"No-o!" the others exclaimed, affecting shock, though I was sure some of their mothers did the washing by hand, but they were enjoying this bit of horror.

"Honest! My father sees it, he collects the rent they owe him every week, and he says it's *filthy* in there and smells awful. They all live *in one room*."

Her friends oohed and aahed again in horror and delight at being so shocked. "Those old miners' cottages by the main crossroad, you mean, Mair?" By the pubs and the police station and the bus stop covered with graffiti.

Maira nodded, her expression full of significance.

I sprang off the desk. "Well I heard what you're saying, Maira," I called. "But isn't it the owner's fault? Isn't it his responsibility? If those poor people he's renting to don't have running hot water and electricity and have to use oil lamps in the evening, shouldn't he put in electricity for them and lay in hot water as the landowner? Isn't that the right thing to do? What he should spend the rent on?"

For the first time I understood that poor old Aunty Beat had no electricity or hot water because someone else had the power to deny them to her, had deemed otherwise. I took a breath, trembling. My cheeks reddened; I was making an utter fool of myself, of course. But.

"My great-aunt lives in one of those cottages."

I'd said it. Admitted something I didn't fully understand, decades ago.

Maira looked startled, no, dumbfounded; she blushed and looked away, pained, but a quick smirk had crossed her face. Well! Kezia Thomas had *relatives* living in those awful dwellings at the Cross that should be pulled down, an eyesore in the community. They went back to Maira's great-grandparents' time. And Kezia had the nerve to stand up for them, attack Maira's father, Mr Glynn (a councillor). Maira's friends pressed round her, confused. I was as confused as them, for I was in awe of Maira and the big house the Glynns lived in on Trissa Road, and her nice ways. Hettie sucked at her straw ferociously, frowning at me, but on my side as we were friends. She was tall and skinny and wore glasses, and was clever and kind. The bell went and the girls shuffled back to their desks, dropping their empty bottles in the crate by the door. Mrs Ellis-Vaughan had arrived, for literature, and we were all terrified of her.

"Wordsworth, gir-r-ls! *Tintern Abbey*, page ninety. '*Thoughts that do often lie too deep for tears.*'"

***

"Their graves is up the 'ill." Dilys pointed ahead past the crematorium in St Peter's cemetery, which was a stone chapel with

"Remembrance" carved over the doorway and a circular stone Celtic cross on the roof. We were climbing the slope to where they lay. We carried a bucket of water each that we'd filled from an outdoor tap provided by St Peter's, and cloths and small brushes to use to scrub the dirt from the crevices in the headstones. I was home on a visit from Canada where I've lived for many years. I'd only been here a week, and this was the only Sunday Dilys said she had free.

The steep hill was strewn with gravestones, some half-buried in the long, rough grass. Drusilla and I must have passed this cemetery many times as children, squeezed in Daddy's sidecar and, later, in his Austin 10, unaware we had relatives buried in the sod in St Peter's, a place we scarcely glanced at. Nobody had told us; children weren't told things then. Great-Granpa and Granma Thomas' graves, in particular, were unknown to us.

"Gorn to 'is early death, Granpa Thomas, after the War," said Dilys morbidly. She meant the Great War. She must have been sixty now, and life had changed for her. The old row of miners' cottages by the Cross had long gone, replaced by a smart glass and steel office building. They'd been an eyesore, their demolition part of the municipal survey, she said. And the old Dilys I remembered in her pinny, her hair pulled up on top of her head screwed into a scarf with wild wisps escaping, her red raw hands scrubbing the washing in the outhouse, had gone with them. Dilys now sported a neat grey perm, a tweed suit and brogues.

She plodded heavily up the path careful not to spill the water over her new shoes, and I followed. Dilys continued talking in a heavy voice, as if to impress me. There'd been improvement everywhere while I'd been away in Canada. People had money, thanks to credit cards, she added gloomily. "Young people gets everything they wants now on credit, Kezia. They're all mountains in debt but nobody cares."

Dilys herself had a council flat out on Llangyfellach Road provided by the municipal government: two bedrooms, a living room, modern bathroom "with *hot* water, *and* a shower," she stressed. A TV, a hi-fi on which she could play Wales' own Katharine Jenkins and Daddy's old records she'd inherited. ("Nobuddy wanted 'em.") The flat also had a gas stove, a gas fireplace – "not as messy as coal" – and a small washing machine in the back hall that she'd been proud to show me. The glint in her eye seemed to imply she'd gone up in the world now, she had the same as in Canada. (No more washboards and mangles and Puritan soap for her.) She'd even learned to drive, and hopped round Swansea in a second-hand Mini Gwilfer had found her. People had better jobs; they didn't wear dungarees to work no more (like Gwilfer). Those days were gone.

"People dun' get buried no more neither, they gets cremated, Kezia. It's cheaper and takes less land and more hygenic." It seemed Nanny Thomas and Aunty Beat were in little receptacles like post office boxes, neat metal containers called urns, slotted in a row inside the Remembrance Wall of the crem. The names of the dead were on the lids, and the year they passed, said Dilys. "Only they ain't called 'the dead' no more. They's 'the deceased'. They dun' die," she puffed and snorted, slopping water from the bucket after all. "They 'passes away'."

People didn't bother with graves no more, neither; she persisted. "They dun' wash graves like us, dun' need to."

But Dilys' life had been the chapel, I recalled, and what did that mean? No make-up, no jewellery, no sex before marriage, thick brown lisle stockings, heavy club shoes, the closest thing to high heels that were not high heels (at least she hadn't worn gum-boots to chapel). She and Nangi and Aunty Beat didn't kneel on hassocks to pray at Ebenezer Chapel as my sister and I did at the Anglican Church. They definitely did not genuflect before the altar – there *was* no altar or cross at Ebenezer, which was a Congregational chapel. "Dun' hold with crosses, dun' hold with angels," Nangi had pointed out the one time Drusilla and I were taken inside, so we would know what it was to be an independent thinker and speak to God directly, without no Pope.

"But I'm not goin' ter be cremated, Kezia, not me. I still wants to be buried in the ground like Great-Granpa Thomas." She looked up at the sky, anxious. Clouds were floating. "No slot in the wall for me, Kezia."

Her plot was already chosen and paid for – "It's over by the hedge," she pointed. Dilys was still a Congregational Nonconformist, who believed in the resurrection of the body, that the body rises whole from the grave. The Congregationals had four ways of proving it. I could only remember "by prophecy", viz Jesus' resurrection, the proof being him walking around Galilee with his dead body raised whole *after* he'd died on the cross, *witnessed* by his disciples, as reported in the New Testament. Nanny Thomas definitely believed that. Dilys said she still believed in the Old Testament too, like the old Covenanters, nonconformists. "*The LORD bringeth death and maketh alive,*" (1 Samuel 2: verse 6), she quoted from the First Book of Samuel. She knew her Bible. She and Aunty Beat and Nangi were quite certain of that; they had conviction. They were not afraid of the words; they were in awe of them. *"Vengeance is Mine saith the Lord."*

But only certain ones were resurrected whole from the grave, to reign with Christ for a thousand years in Heaven: the Chosen, the deserving. ("Those who done good; the bad faces condemnation.") Dilys was definite about that, too; for instance, people who deserted their kin, she hinted.

A slight breeze blew through the long unchecked grasses. It was a pretty hill of trees and bushes scattered with graves and headstones, some of which belonged to our relatives. I knew this now, thanks to Dilys. She remembered, but she was secretive and furtive, guarded, though now I was fifty she was grudgingly more willing to disclose secrets, the whereabouts of the dead. I wanted to know my grandfather Thomas' burial place, and my great-grandfather's and great-grandmother's before him. She was forced to show me, she couldn't very well refuse. I was still family. I was that little girl in a white starched dress holding hands with her twin sister in the sunlight in Aunty Beat's doorway. Dilys grunted assent, her gnarled, veined hands grasped the bucket and she tipped it up over a grave. Water gushed out. Crows flew noisily across the line of trees above. The sky was still blue with puffy clouds; she must have been hot in that tweed suit.

My sister Drusilla had changed too, over the years. She now had dyed blonde hair cut very short, making her look like a boy. She wore glasses – oh, for a long time, "When were you last over?" Faint accusation. She was left with our mother, dealing with Mammy's asthma while I was away living my own life free of it all in Canada. That was what she died of: asphyxiation, despite the oxygen tank. All those cigarettes she'd smoked all her life, even when it became out of fashion, passé.

Drusilla had paused, her lips drawn tight, clenching at her own cigarette – still du Maurier. She offered to take me to the town crem to visit Mammy's ashes, in box 1246 in the Remembrance Wall, very nice. I flinched. Our mother reduced to a little five-by-six-inch receptacle. She'd always been marvellous, tall, majestic, a free thinker.

When I said I was going to help Dilys wash the graves of our great grand-parents at St Peter's Cemetery, Drusilla had stared. "But what on earth *for*, Kezia? We never knew them, and we hardly knew Dilys. Aunty Beat's been dead years. When you're dead you're dead," she challenged.

Not to the Anabaptist Nonconformist Congregationalists, I wanted to say. But I just smiled limply. "Oh-h, I dunno, just to see… find out…" There was always this difference between us as twins.

"Find out *what*?" Drusilla took a jab at the air with her ciggy; it was making her nervous, the unknown. She did not think about things like the bodily resurrection of the dead. She'd forgotten.

"It's…" She struggled for a concept. "… *pagan*! Druid ritual!" she snorted; she always rearranged life. She might be right.

"Well, we are ancient Celts."

"Oh, you always were *dippy*."

It was quiet up there, among the graves. A breeze picked up, wafting through the flowers and grass. I saw my great-grandfather Thomas' grave, on Daddy's side, at last, and Nanny Thomas' father, Great-Grandpa Evans, on her side. Dilys grunted assent, begrudgingly. She didn't really want me there; she was discomfited. I was now this middle-aged, fifty-year-old over from Canada, a foreign land. I left Wales, she hints again. Some time in our teens, Drusilla and I had stopped visiting Nanny Thomas in her shop and going to Aunty Beat's place; perhaps Nangi retired and we never noticed.

It can be frightening, the graves of the dead. There's a sense of whispering through the headstones of the past, peering up through rough blades of grasses and furze.

Dilys put down the bucket at another grave. It seemed a monstrous thing to rub wet cloths over the headstones of relatives. "Yewer great-gran'mother. Haven't bin here a long while, years, what with my chest. It goes to ruin fast."

A word began to emerge on the headstone as I rubbed: M-A-R-K. Mark Evans, Nangi's father, lies beneath the soil. Nearby, Dilys was busy scraping at "Elizabeth", Elizabeth Evans, *wife of... 1824 to...*

There was another grave off by itself, the headstone crooked, buffeted over many years by wind and rain no doubt. I knelt and scraped away the moss and dirt, and slowly a name, D-E-R-E-K, appeared. My cousin Derek. I was surprised. So this was where he'd been all these years. But it was so untended; Dilys had let furze and brambles sprawl over the grey stone, and mosses and lichens matted the headstone. (*That photo of him caught in the sunlight in his plus fours and check shirt that day with his bicycle down Crawley Woods propped against the Toby jug in Aunty Beat's cottage, and the scent of sage and rosemary hanging from the rafters... the sunken old road everyone's forgotten, even Dilys; lost...*)

"That wuz yewer first cousin Derek, Kezia." Dilys' voice began to drone. "But yew wouldn' remember 'im, yew was too little. Died young, only seventeen. Smashed 'is father's car. Stole it to take a *girl* out for a spin what he got in trouble. Never told 'is dad the truth. He got a mate ter fix it behind 'is father's back. But then he got leukaemia; all the lying he done keeping that secret affected 'im, give 'im the cancer."

She paused gloomily, then added with a certain condemnation, the condemnation of the Righteous, "Blood wuz pouring from 'is eyes in the end when 'e died in the 'ospitle. That wuz 'is fate, it was a judgement on 'im," she added, with that certain grim Calvinistic predestination, self-satisfaction, deigned no doubt by the elders of Ebenezer Congregationalist with their black garb and grim, square faces and thin, tight lips. They'd joined the Union of the Anybunwyr in 1925.

I pulled at the furze and flattened the brambles, thorns jabbing my hands which became reddened and raw. Blood and two muddy marks smudged my knees as I knelt over the grave. I tugged fiercely at the tufts of grass, tackled determinedly the dirt embedded in the engraved words. Then I took the bucket of water, what was left, my face obdurate, and swished it with intent over the newly scraped headstone with its hard, cold, comfortless words: *The Lord bringeth death and maketh alive. 1 Samuel 2:6.* I couldn't stop crying. And I still don't know why.

IS THAT THE RIVER CYDNUS?

Glynmor Girls' County Grammar School on the hill had been used as an army barracks during the war rather than the boys' school, which was down in the centre of town and therefore more vulnerable to Hitler's flying incendiary bombs. Our classrooms were of wood, and during the war they had apparently been rigged out with tiered bunks. You wondered if the young soldiers had secretly cried in them at night for their mothers, where we now sat in regulation rows facing the board.

Outside the classrooms, long verandahs ran pleasantly round a central courtyard where we played netball and where, during the war, the new army recruits must have done their drills. The whole school was enclosed by grey stone walls. The boys' school boasted wrought iron railings, the school crest embedded overhead in the gate with crossed swords.

Room 14 faced north. It was a small, stifling room with radiators bubbling hot even in summer. The class monitor regularly had to jump up and loosen a tap on the pipes. There'd be a sudden hiss as if the whole thing was about to explode. We blamed the room, but it was our age; fifteen was a difficult stage in girls, intimated Mrs Ellis-Vaughan, the English mistress, who said such things. She'd toss her blanket over her shoulders. It was what she often wore, a sort of cloak with a mouldy old fringe splattered with booze stains. She taught Shakespeare, grammar and some prose.

"I'll be back in j-ust a minute, gir-rls!" Off for a tipple, no doubt – but a shudder would pass through the room the minute she got back, breathing whisky.

"You there! Third from the back!"

Audrey Evans, who had chosen to sit at the desk behind mine first day of term, was already working her way through a bag of sweets, hard-boils by the sound of crunching going on. She slouched down behind me – why me? – a greenish-looking girl with lank hair and a sneaky smile that hid a mouthful of sweets. Her tunic covered up breasts we'd all seen after gym at showers, big pendulous things that some grammar school boy had squeezed at the bus stop. One day, no doubt, such a boy would take Audrey in his arms and kiss that mouth stinking of liquorice and want to marry her, no matter how spotty she got from all those sweets.

Now Audrey was being dragged to the board by Mrs Ellis-Vaughan, her hard-boils scattering over the floor.

"There, you duffer! There, there, there! A NOUN is the NAME of a PERSON, PLACE OR THING! Five W-H! Who-What-When-Where-Why and HOW!"

Shaken to sobs, Audrey staggered back to her seat, clutching up the hard-boils rolling at our feet, everyone stiff not daring to look at her; nobody wanted her face rubbed like that into the blackboard.

"Now then, gir-r-ls," drawled Mrs Ellis-Vaughan, in a sudden shift of tempo. She had a vivid face, dark curly hair swept up, full lips and flashing teeth, her ears looped with gold rings like a gypsy. "Just remember!" Mrs Ellis-Vaughan paused, smiling now, shifting her blanket: "In the words of Oscar Wilde, Art does not imitate Life. Life imitates Art!"

Macbeth
Act I
Enter Lady Macbeth

Everyone expectant, Audrey chomping again through the thrill of Mrs Ellis-Vaughan's voice declaiming:

"Unsex me here,
And fill me from the crown
to the toe-top full
Of direst cruelty!

Audrey's molars crushed and ground to a sudden halt. Mrs Ellis-Vaughan was going to go through with it, say the words:

"Come to my woman's breasts,
And take my milk for gall!"

Mrs Ellis-Vaughan motioned to her chest and cupped her bosom. Audrey spluttered. Mrs Ellis-Vaughan was pacing by now across the front of the room, our stage, past the rads and the board, her blanket tossed aside – what would she do next? Her voice rose threateningly, causing Miss Mould's Latin next door to tap anxiously on the wood partition: "Is everything all right in there, Mrs E-V?" Of course, ignored. Mrs Ellis-Vaughan was really carried away:

"Come thick night,
And pall thee in the dunnest smoke of hell,
That my keen knife see not the
wound it makes,
Nor heaven peep through the blanket
of the dark,
To cry 'Hold, hold!'"

"Now then, who wants to be Lady Macbeth?" she smiled.

***

Of course, no other teacher could come anywhere near this, least of all Miss Lewis. She was standing in for Mrs Ellis-Vaughan, who had suddenly disappeared (drying out again, no doubt) after the death of Lady Macbeth, leaving the new teacher to cope with our new play, *Antony and Cleopatra*.

Miss Lewis was relatively young and therefore potentially exciting in a staff of mainly old, unmarried women with whispered stories of lost suitors and fiancés in the war. (Some still wore old, tantalising engagement rings on their "engaged" left fingers). But Miss Lewis wore the same beige suits and wedge-heeled shoes as theirs, her hair set in a staid perm. She was going out with someone – a minister with a moustache who drove a Hillman Minx. He picked her up every afternoon after school.

Miss Lewis joined in the hymns at morning prayers in the canteen in a quavering voice: "*Oh God our help in ages past, our hope for years to come, our shelter from the stormy blast...*" She was nervous at register time, making blots in the "present" column and forgetting to collect the absence notes. She actually trembled as she picked up the chalk to illustrate iambic pentameters on the board, her notion of teaching Shakespeare on a long rainy afternoon: "Next, Mair, please."

But we'd been stabbing each other and making love under Mrs Ellis-Vaughan's tutelage for a year – we weren't going to revert to parsing aloud at our desks in rotation. We'd tasted the delights of the boards – "*The play's the thing!*" – that seductive Elizabethan world of role reversals and mistaken identities. Mrs Ellis-Vaughan had had the girls with huskier voices take the male roles, just as the boys in the boys' grammar school played girls' parts. Boys like Vivyan Elton, with his glossy curls and rosebud lips, who took the female lead. Vivyan Elton's mincing treble apparently caught ours perfectly – "*As I am Egypt's queen, Thou blushest, Antony*" – until his voice broke in form three, ending his stardom. Of course, the boys wouldn't admit to their roles as heroines, at the bus stop, any more than we girls would boast about being military heroes. The boys always sniggered, and then pushed you aside in the rush for best seats on the bus. (All the same, you'd have loved to have seen Vivyan's performance just once, but the boys were sealed off with their masters, behind their iron railings, dressed in their maroon and gold blazers, grey trousers and striped school ties.)

Of course, Vivyan would have been the star in the real Globe Theatre of Shakespeare's time, following the great tradition of Elizabethan theatre when women were prohibited from acting. Feted by the spectators, especially the groundlings who paid a penny entrance fee – a rowdy boisterous lot – the pretty boy heroine with the fake bosoms and hips, imitating a girl so beautifully the lewdest groundling would forget heckling and enter that magical pretending. Mrs Ellis-Vaughan had tended to get effusive on the matter – Miss Lewis was terrified of her. We were to understand that Renaissance boys weren't trained to *think* as boys did today, and the wearing of silks and lace ruffles and fineries, singing, playing the lute and making ditties to a mistress were quite *de facto*.

Miss Lewis fluttered at the rostrum, sensing defeat.

"Is that the River Cydnus?" She pointed weakly towards the aisle between our desks.

"Yes, miss. Oh yes."

"What, aisle two?" She was trying to envisage a river running through the classroom.

Anything could happen now in room 14, when *Antony and Cleopatra* ensued and Life imitated Art!

Act II, scene 2: *Music of the hautboys begin now beneath the trapdoor. Entrance of Cleopatra.* Of course, the prettiest girl had been chosen.

Jillian Llewelyn, in school tunic, her regulation tie loosened whimsically at the throat, came sailing down aisle two, the River of Cydnus, fabled of antiquity, past the gurgling pipes as Enid, playing Enobarbus, described Antony's first famous glimpse of Cleopatra, falling in love instantly – we were entranced!

> *"The barge she sat in like a burnish'd throne*
> *burned on the water, the poop was beaten gold,*
> *Purple the sails, and so perfumed that*
> *the winds were love-sick with them…"*

At the four o'clock bell, I stayed back as book monitor to stack the Shakespeares for the teacher, an old Forest of Arden edition with worn red spines. Each girl had an allotted number stamped on the front so the teacher would know at the end of term who had defaced any pages.

I lingered deliberately. Perhaps Miss Lewis might confide in me about her own lovelorn romance. The minister hadn't appeared at the school gates lately. But all that happened was that Miss Tremaine came in to speak with Miss Lewis. I stood to attention; Miss Tremaine was Senior English mistress of the upper sixth. "Please see me later in my work room, Miss Lewis, regarding the syllabus."

Something in her tone, the heavy Victorian slope of her chest, the smooth white curls and firm mouth, exuded an authority that thrilled.

Miss Tremaine glided out as regally as she had entered; she hadn't even noticed me, Kezia Thomas, mere fourth former. She taught Chaucer as well as Shakespeare.

It was still raining out. The yard had that eerie, deserted look as I crossed the verandah and went into the cloakroom. A few odd berets left on hooks, raw walls, and a plastic corrugated roof over the lavatories. The toilet seats were coarse, stinking of blood and leaves, said Enid. She had waited for me, with Gaynor. Audrey Evans was sneaking around behind the pipes somewhere, listening in.

Gay was smoking, thin spirals were wafting round the lav. You could be expelled for it, but she said she didn't care. As "Gay", she dared. She'd been wanting us to call her Gay for weeks now, instead of Gaynor. We all agreed Gaynor sounded goody-goody, which Gay was not. She was into two-inch heels and a duffle coat – see what the prefects would do about that!

I put on my mac, heavy regulation gabardine, and my navy beret with the school crest in front. It made me look even shorter than I was, and stocky. I sighed. The entire uniform with its puffy serge tunic lumping in folds did nothing for me, designed as it was for tall willowy girls like Gay and Enid.

"So did she say anything?"

"Nope," I said, peering in the mirror, a cracked bit of glass over the taps.

Gay was trying to do something with her hair, tease it a bit, also forbidden. It was spiky like a hedgehog's, but you wouldn't dare say. She wanted to go dancing at Eddie's on the weekend, in the Uplands. There was a boy she liked, Rory Jones – "He's smashing, aye!" I wasn't sure. Last time we went, I'd ended up with that boy from Eversley Road, flabby wet lips and all tongue. I shivered.

"Well, are ew coming or what, Kezia?"

Gay meant to Eddie's on Saturday. She was prodding her hair. She wouldn't wear a beret, though it was fifty lines if you were caught.

(But Miss Tremaine was turning towards me, in a new way, in dim room 14, her voice low with recognition...

"You must be Kezia Thomas I've heard so much about, rebel of the lower fourth who never wears her beret."

The pleats of my cute tunic blow gently in the breeze coming in through the open door, wafting from the netball pitch. We stand together, almost touching, teacher, pupil, Miss Lewis forgotten...)

"Wasser marrer with her?"

"She's got a crush – on some teacher in the Forest of Arden," said Enid cleverly.

Secretive Enid, she was Enobarbus in the play, ironic commentator on the fate of others. She was adjusting her beret sideways on her head, as if she were in Paris. Push her face through the glass, with that smirk. Let her think it was Miss Lewis, then.

Enid was not coming to Eddie's Dancing Academy. She was going to spend Saturday night painting herself: "Portrait of the Artiste With Splintered Glasses". She had a thin, sensitive face and wore glasses

At once I felt a stab of regret. I too wanted to be an individualist, and I wasn't.

"Guess what I saw up on the common Sunday afternoon?" I said.

Now that had them, because of course they had to know, except for Audrey Evans who was a Baptist. She read her Bible daily.

"I was lying down, reading a book behind this gorse bush, when…"

Audrey Evans questioned that right away. Lying down in the gorse by myself on a Sunday?? That wasn't right for a girl.

"Shut up, Audrey, let's hear 'er."

The thing that got Enid was their age. Was I *sure* they were old? She'd forgotten she was an artiste. Definitely, Enid, I assured her. He was bald, overweight and wheezy, and *she* was a housewife from the housing estate, someone's mother wearing a coat and headscarf like the Queen. Yet still they had done it, defying danger, unable to control whatever made them burrow down in the scratchy long grass, panting and grasping each other in the gorse. They had a blanket with them and they did it under that, with their clothes still on but loosened, in broad daylight. He was on top at first, and then they switched around and *she* was on top of *him*.

Gay screamed, and Audrey Evans fell down the toilet.

***

… Just the way she walked across the pitch now that the weather had opened up. Gone were the suits. Miss Tremaine was into silk dresses, that soft flowing sort of material with a violet sheen. It clung and swished as she moved towards me. She must feel it, the intensity as we passed each other, nodding across the verandah. *"Eternity was in our lips and eyes, bliss in our brows' bent…"*

"Good morning, Miss Tremaine."

"Oh, good morning."

Miss Tremaine pauses between bells.

"I hear you are quite the leading light of the Shakespeare class, Kezia."

"Oh, not really, Miss Tremaine!"

"Now don't be modest, though it is rather becoming!"

She has a smooth smile, clear green eyes like glass, not unlike the Prioress' in Chaucer's Prologue.

"Perhaps you can visit me one evening, at my home, Kezia. I'd like to hear you do something from the bard. The sonnets, perhaps, under my bed canopy."

"When forty winters shall besiege thy brow..."

Just then, third bell broke over everything.

"Heck whatta yew standing there for like a gawk, staring into space? Come *on*, Kezia, it's singing in the canteen, mun."

***

Miss Tremaine spent much of her day teaching the upper sixth behind glass partitions. In summer she allowed the prefects to sit out on the grass, near the firs by the east verandah.

My eyes followed her from behind the clump of trees where I was hiding, watching as she walked into the sixth form room and settled herself behind the rostrum. Presently, the prefects drifted in, not even noticing the soft blue blouse she was wearing.

Lunch time Miss Tremaine spent in the library catching up on her marking. Sitting at the next table, I pretended to be reading *National Geographic* as she checked exercise books, leaving scrawly marks of red ink across the pages, her face occasionally smiling at something some student had written, her eyes lowered. When she raised them our gaze clasped, startled for an instant.

"What are we always walking down the east verandah for?" said Enid.

Tuesday, second period in the afternoon, Miss Tremaine mended books in the book room. She rebound covers of the Forest of Arden editions, taped broken spines, stamped the name of the grammar school on the first and last pages. If only I could get out of class in period two! It was Shakespeare with Miss Lewis, who was still standing in for Mrs Ellis-Vaughan. If it were Mrs Ellis-Vaughan I might have risked slipping out under pretext of pains.

She might flutter you out with her fingers or scream "Zounds, odds boddikin! Back to thy seat, wench!"

I approached Miss Lewis out on the verandah, waving my Shakespeare with its newly torn spine. "May I take it to the book room, Miss Lewis, to get it mended?"

Miss Lewis was one of those English teachers who, if you said "Can I?" answered: "You can, but you may not."

"A book is the precious lifeblood of a master spirit, Kezia," waived Miss Lewis, from which I conjectured "yes".

You could hear Vera, the monitor, calling from the door where she was on guard, "Miss Lewis is here, you girls, shush. AttenSHUN."

The book room was a secluded space behind the library. I could see Miss Tremaine through the glass door bending over a case stacked with *King Lear*s. She was wearing a lovely floral dress. I realised I had only ever seen her at a certain respectful distance. Now we were to be alone, close together in a small space. I tapped on the glass.

"Yes?"

I closed the door after me and offered the book with its torn spine. Miss Tremaine made a clicking sound with her tongue, sighing over the spine, her hand grasping the book my own still held momentarily. There was a faint scent of eau-de-cologne from her bodice. The warmth of the room was heady, enclosed by books, walls of them methodically stacked alphabetically by her over the years. Such precision had a strange appeal; there was no slacking with Miss Tremaine. This was her hour, period two, in the book room, and somehow that added a little seditious edge: the capricious young girl, the older mistress, fire and air.

"I love you!" I breathed. Then, in a rush from Cleopatra: "*I am air and fire!*"

I was about to add "*My other elements I give to baser life!*" when Miss Tremaine cut in: "Sign here, please."

As I left, she turned momentarily with the cool smile I'd adored. "By the way, Thomas, it's *fire and air.*"

As I reached the verandah, still trembling, I could hear dull Miss Lewis' voice intoning like a dirge: "*I have immortal longings in me*." They must have reached a love scene.

"Ah, Kezia, just in time to play Antony," Miss Lewis said, relieved, as I slipped into my seat, ignoring Audrey Evans behind me sucking something under cover.

I was back in room 14, in that magical – or was it the real? – world of Shakespeare. As Antony I knew what was expected of me. I'd be shorter than Cleopatra, but that didn't matter in front of all girls. They sat in their rows facing the board, flipping their Shakespeares, the restless groundlings on a hot afternoon.

Who would ever know what made Audrey Evans that day stumble down the aisle to be Cleopatra, pleased and overwhelmed. She was in her Pontefract phase again, reeking of liquorice; moreover, she spoke with a lisp:

"Eternity wath in our lipth and eyeth,
Blith in our browth bent…"

Miss Lewis tightened at the rostrum, realising her mistake, too late. But Audrey had been the first to offer – eagerly – and there had been no other.

Marooned out the front by the blackboard, Audrey gasped in fright. Her face was puffy and spotty, her shirt collar fallen open where she had loosened her button. Confused, I swung her in my arms in an awkward embrace not indicated in the text, my teasing Cleopatra!

"Play one thene of exthellent dithembling; and let it look/ Like perfect honour," gulped Audrey, startled as I pulled her to my breastplate, like a lump of dough. ("*You'll heat my blood no more!*") In the struggle, her mouth pressed unexpectedly into mine, soft and squishy and open. Ugh-h. Audrey's book fell with a plop.

"Oh, pleathe mith…" she cried at astonished Miss Lewis, in the excitement of the moment.

***

Already it seemed a century away, lost like actors in a dream, hiding a deeper sorrow. For what I puzzled over as the years went by was not Miss Tremaine's rejection, understandable, but that she hadn't felt the magic – the music of the hautboys – fire and air! – *"I am again for Cydnus… sirrah!"* And Audrey had.

LAST NIGHT WHEN WE WERE YOUNG

"So how old are you, then?"

He was tall, the tallest in Eddie Hewton's Dancing Academy in Swansea. And he'd chosen me for the quickstep – s*low-slow* – *quick-quick* – He had hard eyes and a hard body.

"Seventeen," I said quickly, too quickly perhaps. I'd learned to add a few years to my age when with an older boy – he looked at least twenty. Otherwise he might think you too young for doing whatever it was would happen in his arms.

It was the Saturday night bop at Eddie's, a long, brightly lit hall next to the tavern in the Uplands. It cost five shillings entrance fee. Every Saturday, young men – chaps – came down from the valleys to pick up girls in our seaside town. They said we were prettier, faster than the quiet, dull girls up in the hills, places with names like Ystalyfera or Lower Cwmtwrch.

"Hmm." He didn't believe me, you could tell.

He wheeled me round and the frothy petticoat under my floral dress frilled out in the faces of a row of girls sitting out down the side, ones who hadn't been asked. They sat stiffly on hard-backed chairs against the wall, pretending to be enjoying themselves, their faces hot and flushed and edgy. Mitzi was one of them, but she stood defiantly, staring straight ahead. She hadn't been asked and I had, and for one moment I felt that exhilaration of the chosen that a boy's attention gave you. But I was sorry for Mitzi, the way her eyes blazed as if she were intently interested in something going on the other end of the floor, a ploy I used myself.

It was Mitzi who'd pushed me to come. "There's smashing boys, aye, Kezia," she'd said after Latin, Friday afternoon. "And you never know who you might meet." She winked. And surely I was pretty enough.

She'd helped me with my translation, *Caesar in Gallo omnia vincit...* It was the part where Julius Caesar puts out the eyes of ten thousand Gauls in the Gallic Wars. Strange, all the military history we girls had to memorise. (Catullus' love poetry was deemed inappropriate, *"Mille et decem mille bacci, tua lingua..."*, *"A thousand, ten thousand kisses, your tongue..."*)

Mitzi was tall and slim, and tops in Latin, but of course she never let that on to boys.

"All those young, Celtic men blinded by Julius Caesar," I'd mourned. "Their eyes burned out with hot irons." Two thousand years ago.

"Cripes! Forget Caesar's bloody Gallic Wars, Kezia, or you'll never get asked!"

Now she was the one sitting out.

The good-looking boy, the only smasher who'd ever asked me, said, "Don't talk much, do you? Cat got your tongue?"

I hated it when boys said things like that. Who did they think they were?

"I was remembering a story I read in class, about the Romans," I said feebly. Now, of course, I had to go on. "The vestal virgins tending the sacral fires in Rome were really temple prostitutes, it said in the addenda," I added.

That was it. Absolutely the wrong response – *slow-slow – quick-quick* – Mitzi would choke.

My partner rolled his eyes towards the ceiling. "Oh, a brainer."

Next moment, I was back on the sidelines, on a hard chair. The band struck up a rumba, and I saw him moving towards a very pretty girl with masses of curls and asking her for the next one. *"Put your head on my shoulders..."*

I blinked hard. Now I had to sit and wait as boys shuffled round the edge of the girls sitting out, looking you over, the way they do. You were supposed to say "yes" to whoever asked you, but sometimes you could get away with, "Oh, I'm sitting this one out, thanks," and then you had to, even if a dreamboat came along, said Mitzi. If you didn't, they took it out on you. Mitzi never missed a Saturday.

"So what's 'is name?" Mitzi was excited.

But I didn't know.

"What d'you mean you don't *know*?"

"I didn't ask," I said, quickly adding: "He's not my type. I gotta go to the ladies' room." Another stand-by. Mitzi agreed; she wanted to freshen her lipstick, top up her mascara. She had on false eyelashes for a lark, they looked like brushes.

The toilets were jammed with girls powdering their cheeks in the long mirror; hot, sickly sweet smells arose. The mirror ran the length of the wall, with a row of basins and taps. One girl was putting cotton pads in her armpits. "I don't half sweat, aye," she said.

Another girl was going on: "… and he said to me he was in Cadets and I thought, oh brilliant! I loves a uniform… and it turns out he meant Cadet Cleaners. Simpled, aye." And her pretty face blushed, hiding the disappointment and mortification. "Oh well!" She dropped him like a hot cake, of course, not to give him ideas.

A big girl called Pam sat in the corner in tears; she hadn't been asked. Every week she came in a lovely ruched organza dress, her hair back-combed and sprayed. She stood blinking bravely on the sidelines dance after dance and never got asked, not even for a cha-cha. Too anxious, said Mitzi. It didn't do to seem too eager, boys didn't like that. She flicked her eyelashes with black, stiff stuff that made them stick out like bristles.

What boys liked, and what boys didn't like. Fast girls, loose girls, but sweet and nice at the same time. You knew what "nice" was, but that didn't necessarily get you walked home, the proof of being chosen, singled out from the other girls. It could lead to

French kissing and who knew what, hinted Mitzi, and then she would gurgle and you were supposed to fill in the rest yourself. Mitzi was technically a virgin – she'd stressed "technically" with a little secretive smile – and you were supposed to know what that meant too.

I put on fresh lipstick; "*Tender Moment*" it was called.

"You should try '*Allure*'," said Mitzi.

Touch of imitation "*Revien*" from Paris behind my earlobe, and my mother's string of pale glass beads round my throat to set off my rosy cheeks. I was "nice".

Back on the floor you could hear the band starting up. *"Last night when we were young…"*

There was the cha-cha, the rumba, the samba, and a new kind of dancing that fast girls did. They called it jiving and bopping, and you didn't need a boy for a partner. Two girls danced together facing each other, jiggling their hips in school in the dinner hour; they would dance practising until the bell. Someone brought in a record player and there they were, the desks pushed back, a swarm of girls in a circle clapping to the beat while Bessie Morgan and Elsie Evans bopped furiously, their knees bent, tunics twirling. They wore white ankle socks and light slip-on shoes instead of the heavy regulation Oxfords. Bopping shoes were with it. You didn't need boys for jive and bop, boys didn't take you in their arms and hold you close and lead you round the floor.

But you *wanted* to be in someone's arms. You did, and you didn't – everything you'd heard about.

"I falls in love too easily…" sighed a pretty, plump girl.

It was all about falling. "I could fall for 'im big time, aye," said Mitzi, but he didn't ask her, he was asking me again.

"Dance?"

Being led out there past the rows of girls and their scent and powder and anxious sweat. It could only mean one thing: I must have intrigued him after all. Dazed, I smiled brightly, eagerly, gratefully, forgetting Mitzi's cautions. He was good-looking, blond, and he'd chosen me. *Slow-slow – quick-quick –*

"You're sweet, a bit dotty but nice. Bet you're not a day older than fifteen."

He squeezed my arm and smiled: a keen, swift, summing-up sort of smile, as if I'd do. This time I merely nodded, still dazed. He was holding on to me, his arm around my back possessively, as the band gave a last blast. This meant he wanted to go on with the set, maybe the next and the next, and even ask to walk me home.

"Last call, last dance," went the MC eventually. And I didn't have to worry. It was happening, and I was surprised how smoothly I was manoeuvred in his arms, accepting it as my due as the coloured ceiling lights whirled above pink, violet, mauve, blue, the band shifting mood to the last slow sad one. *"Unforgettable, that's what you are, Unforgettable though near or far... That's why, darling..."* The left-over girls trailed slowly back to the ladies'.

His name was Something Matthews. Sounded like Roland, Roland Matthews. I thought of him as Mr Matthews.

The thrill of walking down the steps to the girls' cloakroom, whispering so he wouldn't hear my excited *"He's walking me home!"* I wouldn't be catching the bus with Mitzi and the others now. They were taking the number ten home at the corner.

Mitzi nudged Valerie and Rhonda James as they pulled on their coats, and they glanced at me slyly. They'd want to know all about it in school Monday morning, before the bell. "Kezia Thomas went home with a real smasher." It would be all over the lower fourth.

Of course it was different outside. It was raining, with a mist sneaking up from the sea. I didn't have a mackintosh. The bus went by, and I just caught sight of Mitzi and the girls sitting on the side seats laughing, ghostly through the misted-up window.

My stilettos clacked on the hard pavement.

Soon I was hobbling; I couldn't help it, three-inch heels hurt.

Mr Matthews kept his arm round my waist and we walked lopsidedly up the road. I barely reached his shoulder, but there was no one to see it now, no envious girls. It was a long walk to the council house estate, and then up Linden Hill where I lived. I worried my curls would drop from the damp. Some were already falling frizzy on my face. I wouldn't be what he thought I was, bubbly curly-tops, sweet little thing.

Mr Matthews didn't seem to mind my not talking anymore. He was breathing heavily up the hill when he pulled me suddenly into a bus shelter, for a kiss. "In here, love."

He hadn't asked my name yet, only, "You're a nice girl, I can tell."

And then, in an expert way Mitzi never told me about, he leaned me against the wall of the shelter and began kissing, but not like a grammar school boy. A big, greedy swallowing with his tongue. Suddenly he looked older, much older. Now he was breathing fast and his eyes looked funny, concentrated. I jerked my face away, wanting to cry, and there was a bit of a tussle. My beads broke and trickled down my chest, *oh-h*.

One hand had me gripped in an expert way while the other was pulling at my panties swiftly between my legs. I could see an old couple through the misted-up glass walking up the other side of the road, the only people around out there; they were shuffling slowly carrying an umbrella. To them we'd be just a couple of young lovers having a bit of fun in the bus shelter on a Saturday night. They walked on slowly into the mist averting their gaze, heads down.

"I got to be home by twelve, my father's out there waiting for me." I tried to sound calm, keep calm. *I'm only in lower fourth,* I wanted to cry.

"Oh you won't be late, dearie, I promise," he whispered, his breath coming faster. "This won't take a minute," he gasped, pushing himself hard against my belly. "You just be a nice, good little girl."

PWLL DU

"How do I look, kiddo?"

Mother twirled about the living room in the new pink dress she'd just finished sewing. It had black rickrack edging to show off the delicate pink flowers, tiny, sweet flowers of summer. The skirt was on the short side to show off her long legs.

"Lovely, Mum."

"Do I look thirty-nine?" My mother's face puckered anxiously. "Now, be honest!"

"Oh no! You look young." What was young? I was sixteen but felt older than Mother.

Mother gave another exuberant flounce round the sofa. The large front window overlooked the steep street outside; anyone walking by could look in and see. The dress freed something in her, she laughed, something physical I only sensed. I'd never show myself off in such a way, so openly like Mother; I'd hide my pleasure at my body as I so often had to when she was fitting a dress on me. She'd run her hands over me, pressing the material in place, here and there, over my breasts lightly – "Keep still" – her mouth full of pins, to check the fit of the bodice. I'd tremble indignantly, struggling to keep a firm expression on my face. "There, a nice fit" she'd say blandly.

She put on natty little sandals to match.

The other mothers on Linden Hill wore shapeless pinafore dresses they did their housework in, something Mother disdained;

she was the only mother on the council estate who went out to work, out into the world of men. They'd look at her admiringly, wonderingly. "There goes Mrs Thomas," as she click-clicked down the road in the mornings in a waft of perfume. Off to the office, leaving them behind and my sister and me to lock up. The key was kept in the outdoor lavatory to let ourselves in after school.

"Well, let's go then, chicks."

The Sunday afternoon walk, up over the common and down into one of the bays then back through the Mumbles, a five-mile circuit. I was in a quandary. I too wore a lovely homemade dress of shimmering cotton Mother had run up for me, hardly suitable for walking round the cliffs, but Mother loved it. "That dress is my magnum opus!" She was the only mother on the street to quote Latin. It was a dress to be seen in (though by whom?) at some special event, the friends of Mother's youth invariably met along the way. They'd comment, with implication surely, "There's Mrs Thomas with her daughter, Kezia," or, sometimes, "with her clever daughter."

So I too had to look lovely, do Mother proud. High heels would be agonising. I decided on flat slip-ons.

"You're not wearing those?"

"Well, they're comfy for round the cliffs."

Mother appraised me coolly a moment, her eyes passing over my body; I wished I could hide.

"You're so *short*! A little half-pint!" she joked, looking down at me amused as we set out, arm in arm up the hill. On either side were close-packed council houses with netted windows and often potted geraniums on the sills. *"There goes…"*

And where was my sister Drusilla on this hot afternoon? Certainly not walking across the common with her mother. "Huh, you wouldn't catch me doing that!" In her new secret push-up bra like a ribbed cage pressing her tits forward for the boys to ogle. She was going out with Tony Hancock – Toe-Knee-Hand-Cock – the fastest boy in the village, whom she'd met after church one Sunday in the coffee shop. I knew. After church a year ago, one winter night, four of us girls had gone off after evensong with four boys, partnering up under the boats in the harbour in the Mumbles. It was dark under the boat, with a tang of seaweed and wet sand. A distant boom of waves round the pier.

"It's nice in here out of the wind, no one can see us," the boy I was with had said. He had curly hair and bubbly lips. I'd lain down obediently on the cold sand under the ribs of wood. He'd opened my coat and slid his hands over my breasts under my jumper and kissed me, soft wet kisses, and I'd thought, *I'm being kissed by a boy, this is what it's like*. His hand had known what to do. It hurt. It went straight to a place and poked about not unpleasantly like a hard little stick.

I'd tried to see what Drusilla was doing with Toe-Knee; there was a flurry of clothes in her corner and a "ugh-ugh-ugh". "Your sister's not half goin' at it," said the boy I was with, Vernon was his name. "Wasser marrer with you then?"

I recalled Mother earlier standing in Drusilla's way in the hall. "And where d'you think you're going on a Sunday afternoon, my girl?"

Drusilla had pushed past her. "Out."

As soon as she was gone, Mother went upstairs and tore open the clasp of Drusilla's diary hidden under her pillow. "Just as I thought!" She read excitedly the words Drusilla had written. "Disgusting! They're doing everything." Then, in anger: "She won't have anything left to find out on her wedding night."

How much more did a boy do on a "wedding night"? I didn't know and mother did. Drusilla did, too.

"Mam, you shouldn't be reading her diary," I protested. "It's private."

"I'm her mother." Mother went to the laundry box and found Drusilla's knickers and sniffed them, something she often did, a secretive look on her face.

So Drusilla was gone for the afternoon, first sneering at me, "Little Miss Priss, you wouldn't stand up to Mammy for anything!"

Mother's arm was tight in mine as we braced for the hill. After a moment, she started up conversation.

"You know what that Mr Williams opposite said to me the other day about you, Kezia?" she began in a low, intimate way. "He had the nerve to say wasn't I worried about you, you've never had a boyfriend, it's not normal a girl your age; cheeky bugger."

My cheeks burned, as much at Mother's bemusement as at Mr Williams' invasion of my privacy.

"So what did you *say*?" I tried to hide my agitation. I was an anomaly, then, to the neighbours. They'd noticed something about me, perhaps my satchel of books bulging on my back after school each day. Yes, it was a cheek, a frightful cheek of him. But what did he see about me that might be true? I gripped my little matching purse that was supposed to bring out the colour of my dress.

"Oh, I just said Kezia's not interested in boys right now, she's far too intelligent. But one day, when Mr Right comes along…"

Mother paused. This future fiancé would be someone special, given it was me. I stumbled on the rocky path. Linden Hill had given way to a stony lane at the top that led to the common. Trees bent overhead, then suddenly parted. Oh, the open moorland!

Everything was worth this. The vast open space. Far below was the housing estate nestled into the hill, and the sea below that dazzling blue, iridescent with meaning, around the Mumbles Pier. Across the common, invisible cliffs showered down to the shore, the sparkling bays like necklaces.

Up here all was bright and golden, the gorse popping in the hot sun. A cow grazed in the distance, a dot on the horizon; the grass burned and scratched our ankles.

"God's own country!" breathed Mother, in her new wedge-heels. We linked arms for a while, not all the time because Mother's weight was heavy and I barely reached her shoulder.

"There's always one child who's closer to you," Mother sighed happily, giving me a squeeze.

I was now that child, a confidante. I had my mother all to myself, special in a way Drusilla never would. I felt a brief pang of doubt, a dark thudding, the way a shadow ripples out of nowhere under a hot blue sky or a current sucks at you beneath the calm surface of things.

A lark broke through the clear blue sky the way larks do, its cry invisible, piercing the silence.

"We're more like sisters, Kezia." Mother tucked my arm in hers again, happily. There was the dark thudding still behind the sunlight. Where was Drusilla that very minute? Off with her friends in the village enjoying herself, having an ice cream in Forte's Parlour with her boyfriend? Vaguely I felt dissatisfaction. What was I doing at sixteen, being a companion to Mother?

There was silence for a while. Then: "Oh I've got some more talk for you from the office! We do have a good time at work, aye. Oh the jokes, the things they say!" I tensed. Mother glanced at me sideways tentatively. "They're a bit on the blue side."

I hesitated shyly, yet willing to hear of the secret talk of women, this other world of Mother's office, of working women, that I too would belong to one day.

"It was something Beryl said yesterday in the office to that silly Phyllis." Beryl was an older typist, married. Young Phyllis Cheyney, only a year older than myself, was reputedly "after" Mr Lloyd, the boss, as I well knew from Mother's tales. I could see her in my mind, young and pert, fresh out of school in her first clerk-filing job, clicking into the office in the Maritime Chambers where Mother worked in a wave of perfume and jingling earrings and tight, lacy tops. The others, the older married women like mother – and Beryl – watching, advising, enjoying.

Mother continued, amused, affecting shock: "… and that shameless Beryl called out to Phyllis as she was leaving to meet her boyfriend in the Strand – oh she has a tongue on her – 'Remember, Phyllis, a standing cock knows no conscience.'" Mother tittered.

I kept my face to the horizon far away where the lark had called.

Mother pulled away her arm, annoyed. "Well, Miss Priss, why the look? Oh don't tell me you don't *know* what it means!"

What was it about myself I didn't understand? Mother was so tall and magnificent. I pushed back the disappointment.

A few clouds hovered overhead, nothing to worry about. Mother was well away again, on to the topic of Olwen Sweeney. And once again I listened, fascinated, an ugly fascination for something being revealed through someone I could be, for I recognised in Olwen, of course, my alter ego. Olwen Sweeney, the virgin of the village, still under her mother's control at twenty-seven. The Sweeneys were an old Mumbles family tracing their lineage back to the Vikings – but who really cared, I thought. Would a man care? Not just any bloke would do for Olwen; he had to come from the right background, the right public school and have something called "old" money.

"Oh Mrs Sweeney's keeping her on ice, all right," Mother confided. ("Let's hope she doesn't freeze over permanently or he'll have to use a pickaxe on the night," she tittered again.)

I winced, yet wanted to hear more, more women's dirty, titillating talk. The sky above spread out hot and blue and sultry; the sea was far away and had changed, the tide had turned and was going out, a rippling line across the vast sands. Mother was Mrs Sweeney's confidante. They had recently taken a weekend office trip to Llandrindod Wells where they'd been a threesome, Olwen trailing dutifully along with the two older women, to take the waters. Mrs Sweeney still believed in chaperones. After all, they were descended from Vikings.

"Kezia, you just wouldn't believe!" cried mother. "Olwen still wears homemade cloth napkins held up with safety pins – you know, at 'that time'. And Mrs Sweeney *stands over her* in the toilet watching while she changes. Honest, I couldn't believe it! And Olwen twenty-seven!"

I felt the deep thudding again, the sky closing in. For I could see Mrs Sweeney, a First Mumbles Baptist, powerfully chested, breathing over Olwen fumbling with her homemade sanitary napkin under her mother's gaze, Olwen's confusion. I looked sharply at Mother but she was striding confidently over the furze, unaware, as always, supremely secure in my loyalty. *"We're like sisters, we two, Kezia."* The memory of my own first menses bubbled up hot and wet and shameful. I'd sat on the sands at Langland Bay that summer day, the large wet spludge of blood spreading across my white shorts as I walked back to the car, everyone seeing. How could I hide it from my father?

The secret was passed on. Mother showed me the Kotex napkins, the bulky pads I was now to wear secretly between my legs every month, held up by an ugly elastic belt, until I was forty. I would follow my flow like the pull of the moon's power over the sea (the same power in the universe), month by month in a secret cycle boys did not have. (This secret must definitely be kept from Father and Davey and Toe-Knee-Hand-Cock).

"Time for your bath," Mother had said that Sunday night as usual.

Oh, but I have my period, but I couldn't say the word as Daddy was nearby, sitting in the armchair.

"It's your turn."

Drusilla and I bathed separately now we were "young ladies", as Mother said.

"But I'm fourteen, can't I bathe myself? Trisha Matthews does."

Mother ran the water, got down the flannel and soap and loofah. "Hurry up, take off those clothes."

My breasts were small and tight with pink aureoles, and I tried to hide the bush of black hair down below with my hands. Obediently, I crouched in the shallow water she'd run – a few inches to save on water, you'd think it was still wartime. "Now wash properly down there!" Mother watched, standing at the edge of the tub, and I closed my eyes and dabbed and my mother was amused. "Properly!"

How long did it go on? Age twelve, thirteen, fourteen. By fourteen I rebelled. But Mother would have continued, perhaps until I was twenty-seven, like Olwen: "Take off your clothes."

"I won't! I want to bathe myself with the door shut!" I meant *locked.* Tight, angry words – Drusilla had long ago simply pushed mother aside on Sundays and slammed the door in her face, "I'm bathing myself!" – "Just *tell* her, Kezia, the old cow!" she'd shot at me.

Something had come to an end for Mother. I locked the door and removed my dress, more slowly my underthings. Then I lay in my nakedness in the bath water for the first time, looking shyly at the forbidden, and so much more.

***

We had reached the headland, the common behind us already forgotten. For we had reached Pwll Du – "Black Pool" – and at once the afternoon opened into something else. Far below, the bay, the most secret, inaccessible of coves, circled by its towering cliffs only the insane would attempt, Mother loved to say. We began the descent.

The narrow, rocky path, a mere ledge in places at the edge of the precipice, wound round the cliff, the sea below, chaffing. "You need to be a ruddy goat!" snorted Mother. Waiting for the moment you knew was coming, that second at the last turn and you were poised as if mid-air between rock and sky, the bay suddenly there deep in the basin, the cliffs rising above stiff and towering, wet with spume. When the sun lowered behind the cliffs later in the day, the bay would become a dark, black pool, mysterious, foreboding, and you shivered.

The beach was like no other: waves of white shingle through which a thin stream curled like a snake from the woods above the valley.

Our feet crunched across the stones until we had to cross the wooden footbridge. The stream was deeper there, quite deep, and the water dark green. Mother fluttered, affecting a girlish voice, as always, belonging to her girlhood. "Oh this is where I was always afraid to cross and I'd say 'Dada, I'm frightened!' and he'd always pick me up in his arms and carry me over."

Mother, afraid of something? Impossible. Yet it was so.

Now the sea was hidden for a while; the path widened becoming sandy and lovely and soft and sheltered. It meandered and we came to the old, deserted house on the left that had been an almshouse in its day, in Mother's childhood, for this is where we were, in her girlhood past. "Pwll Du Alms" it had been called, now covered in wild flowering vines and trailing, passionate flowers wet with spume. The roof and porch had long since caved in, the lead-paned windows cracked and grimy. The garden burst with a profusion of blossoms run wild, musk roses and dogwoods and lupins and honeysuckle. There was a steady buzz of bees.

Opposite stood an equally dilapidated structure, an old long-deserted cottage with broken boards. Outside were long, shaky trestle tables and benches, bleached and split, and a faded signboard: "Rees' Tea Rooms." Mother sighed. Mrs Rees was still alive. "God, she must be ninety-five if she's a day!"

Mrs Rees was in (where else would she be?), peering through a crack in the door as if expecting us. She would have heard our steps crunching across the shingle.

She remembered Mother, peering up at her. "Mavis Norman! Well, well." She smiled an old toothless smile and beckoned us in.

It was dark and cool in the one room, a parlour with an old iron hob and black walnut settle by the window like so many old Welsh cottages. There was a dark oak Welsh dresser in a corner filled with china never used.

A cat staggered on five legs across the linoleum, then a weak furry ball, and another stumbling blind one. "Cats 'ave 'ad kittens," said Mrs Rees hoarsely, apologetically.

Again. There was a lean-to out in the scullery, and Mrs Rees tried to shoo them out there, "Out out! *Allan!*"

"Oh, can't I see them?"

"You dun' want to see them, dearie."

But I did. I did and I didn't want to, to look; the ugly fascination for the darkness, the obscene that such, surely, was in me? I pushed the door ajar, affecting innocence. It was so dark in there with a glance of sunlight through a crack in the boards. Mrs Rees' storage place was filled with bins and sacks of dried and canned food. Over the floor, mewling and staggering, lay the kittens of the mother cat – if such she was – for I'd long figured out she could be her own offspring's sister or grandmother or aunt. Perhaps her own son had straddled her one frenzied afternoon driven by need, and how would she know? I shut it out at once, the image, but it was undeniable; generations of cats and kittens, fathers copulating with daughters and granddaughters and sisters and mothers and sons. It was what happened in nature, if you let it, and you tightened but you still looked.

All were blind and deformed. Some had three testicles, swollen and strange, like gourds dragging to the ground. They crept into the parlour on their bellies, one with an extra useless limb grown out of its leg. Why? That was the question. Why did she allow it?

Mrs Rees sighed and said in a weak voice, "What can I do?" She pushed the kittens behind a curtain hanging on brass rings. "Have to get the supply boy to drown 'em." But you knew she wouldn't.

"Remember all the teas out the front, Mrs Rees, all the sandwiches, in the old days…?" Mother was sipping a cup of tea.

"Oh aye."

The kitten with three eyes slumped by the hob; it couldn't find its mother.

"Why doesn't she get them fixed and put a stop to it?" I demanded later as my mother and I walked to the shore. Had Mammy seen them? She surely had.

"Oh-h, well, it's not so easy, I suppose, living down here all alone and isolated all year."

"How does she live then?" What did she eat? I'd never wondered before about Mrs Rees; she was always just there, part of the rocks, of the deep pool.

"Well, supplies are hauled down once a month, not at all in winter," said Mother vaguely. Down the cliff face to old Mrs Rees below, her lifeline. No electricity, no phone. "Why d'you want to know all of a sudden?"

"Where does she get water from?" I persisted, perturbed.

"There's a secret well up the cliff only she knows about, the last living person. She won't give it away for love nor money."

"But she could be dying and no one would know." With the deformed monsters around her.

"Oh well, she's thought of that, I suppose." Mother was getting evasive, this was off-topic, disturbing. "She was a lovely young woman once. All those teas in high season, the mounds of sandwiches, the cream slices..." The sun had moved across the sands.

"But don't you think she's sick? That it's... *abnormal.*" I struggled to express it, what it was I wanted my mother to acknowledge, to admit, face up to, but she wasn't listening. For the sea was upon us, and the rocks shining. The deep black pool of Pwll Du trembled among the shingle. The waves lifted, a wall of foam in a wondrous way. There was hardly anyone around – we had it all to ourselves, Mother breathed. All of it.

THE SOUND OF THE SEA
AT THE BOTTOM OF THE HILL

I was sitting on the windowsill outside Nanny's house in town one Saturday morning, smiling to myself. I was reading a story by Dylan Thomas in his book *Portrait of the Artist as a Young Dog*. It had a funny title: "Just Like Little Dogs". It was about these two young men hanging out with Dylan on a wet Saturday night under the arches, smoking and staring at the sea. The men did this every evening to escape their wives at home, the twist of fate, the twist of love I couldn't yet imagine at fifteen – that you could end up by accident with the wrong partner, stuck for life, with only a Players cigarette and a penniless poet for company on the Swansea sands.

I actually knew those sands, the way they stretched vast and flat with ripples of dunes behind and coarse grass and the Mumbles Pier dimly emerging through mist. Nanny's house on Western Street was but a walk away down a long, terraced road that led straight to the sea at the bottom. At neap tide the water would come rushing up, a luminous wall shining and brilliant and dangerous, and Nanny got out the sandbags. But Dylan did not have it like that; his sea was muted and melancholy with a loneliness I recognised.

"What on earth are you doing sitting out here like this, a big girl like you!" said Nanny crossly, amazed. She'd come out to check the letterbox. What would the neighbours think?

I snapped the book shut and followed her in, my school satchel bulging with books. I was in fourth form at the girls' grammar school. Spending the night with Nanny was supposed to be a treat.

My Oxfords clacked down the long, dark passage to the middle room. Everything was blinding dark after the sunshine, but you dared not switch on a light; Nanny was always saving electricity even though the war had been over for decades.

"Don't put on the light!" warned Nanny. "I'm not Andrew Carnegie."

The middle room was as gloomy as the rest of the house. One long, sashed window overlooked a cobbled yard at the back with a high wall the neighbourhood cats ran along. I put down my satchel and followed Nanny into the scullery, a long, dreary room, icy and forbidding, smelling of carbolic soap. There was a deep, porcelain sink with two iron taps by a cracked window, offering another view of the yard: the wall, full length. The kitchen still had a stone floor. Nanny was in the middle of making Welsh cakes for our morning elevenses. I was supposed to be helping and learning. I fed in the currants.

"Well, fancy you reading *him*," she scoffed. The cover of *Portrait of the Artist* featured a rugged-looking Welsh miner type with curly black hair and roguish blue eyes, nothing like the photos I'd seen of the real Dylan, with pudgy baby cheeks and a bulbous nose. In the background was a vague impression of Swansea town with smoking chimney stacks, nothing like the real town which had the beautiful blue bay.

"Young dog he was, too – and a lot else!"

"But Nanny, it's *Dylan Thomas*." I was shocked. Our very own world-famous Welsh poet and story writer, who'd lived up the road from Nanny's by Cwmdonkin Park. She'd sometimes taken my twin sister Drusilla and me there as children, for sedate Sunday walks. Of course, Cwmdonkin in the Uplands, with its quiet tree-lined street and semi-detached villas with names like "Sea View" could hardly be compared with the Sandfields where Nanny lived. Western Street housed Hancock's brewery with its pungent stench of hops and dust and something else, a greyness that Dylan rhapsodised as his "ugly lovely town".

"*Ych a fi*!" Nanny slapped down a dollop of batter on the griddle. There was no translation for this Welsh exclamatory. Again, I was flustered.

"But Nanny, there's the most killing story in it about these two young men in love with two girls they get pregnant one night on the sands. But they switch partners halfway through in the dark, and they don't know whose kid is whose and so they end up having to marry the wrong girl. It ends with the judge in the case wagging his finger and saying 'Just like little dogs!'"

Nanny stared. "Is that what they're teaching up at the grammar school these days?"

"Oh, it goes deeper than that, of course. It's also about... passion." I hesitated.

"Well, *that* don't last, I can tell you!" Nanny slapped down another dollop of pastry, intimating danger ahead for any young girl about to embark on the experience, as if she expected me to know. And I didn't. I'd only so far liked Miss Cranmer, the new English mistress for Shakespeare at school. Fair hairs ran like dust down her arms I imagined brushing lightly with my lips. Silly, of course. She'd said, "You have a musical ear, Kezia, a poet's ear." I'd felt a quick pleasure akin to a rush of waves...

... a rush that Nanny must have felt for Granpa once, as a coquettish eighteen-year-old bride with hair to her knees marrying a thrilling businessman thirteen years her senior; dear old Gramps who used to sit in the armchair by the fire with a tankard of beer after a long day's drudge in the bakery and two world wars. Is that what she meant?

"Look sharp," said Nanny. She was expecting company: her oldest neighbour and friend, Miss Dinsmore from Tawe Street.

We set the table as if for the queen. Nanny was bent over like a hoop, with her widow's hump. She had a woolly tea cosy on her head and a string of pearls round her neck. She put out lace doilies.

I peered inside the dresser for the crystal decanter. The shelf was dark and musty, the wood old walnut. At the back were two faded post office savings books Nanny had been filling with stamps every week since the war, for Drusilla and me, in readiness for our trousseaux. I quickly filled the decanter with sherry, laid out dinky silver teaspoons, crystal sugar pot. I was debating whether to tell Nanny that Dylan Thomas had also written some of the greatest poems in the world. "Death Shall Have No Dominion", with the line *"Dead men naked we shall be one With the man in the wind and the west moon."* Instead, I said out loud about another poem, called "Fern Hill", about his childhood. Really, I thought, about childhood lost. I recited: *"Time held me green and dying, though I sang in my chains like the sea."*

Nanny was amused.

"Well he certainly chained himself to the bar of every pub in Swansea. They should 'ave thrown away the key. He tried to make out with Aunty Blod once in the Pavilion, if you please!"

"Aunty Blod?"

"Look at you now," said Nanny, startled. "Getting all excited over something like that." How would I ever get a husband?

But I couldn't contain my excitement and pride. Dylan Thomas had actually been after my Aunty Blod in the dance hall up the road!

"She gave him what for. Cheeky bugger."

So furthermore Dylan Thomas had been rejected by an aunt of mine. (But Aunty Blod! She was fat and blousy and would say at Christmas she fancied cockles, bursting into fits of mystifying laughter, and everyone would say, shocked, "Oh Blodwen!")

"Don't look like that. Our Blodwen was a beauty in her time."

Just then the doorbell rang. It was Miss Dinsmore, come for morning tea and a sip of sherry.

Miss Dinsmore, Nanny's oldest neighbour and friend from the war, was rightly Mrs Parry, but her husband Wilfred had died so long ago the neighbours had reverted to her maiden name of their childhood, as was often the custom.

Miss Dinsmore settled herself in nicely by the fire. She was dressed in black and kept her black felt hat on throughout, with a jewelled pin thrust through the brim like a dagger.

"A little of what you fancy, Flo?" said Nanny.

"Don't mind if I do, Emmie. Medicinal purposes," tittered Miss Dinsmore. "Ooh, is that fresh Welsh cakes I smell?"

"Bring in the platter from the scullery, Kezia. This is my granddaughter, you haven't seen for a while. She's staying the night with her old gran, for company."

"Pretty girl," I heard from the scullery. "And is she courting?" added Miss Dinsmore slyly.

"Oh, Kezia's going to the university and then she'll be off abroad. Make the most of her chances we never got, Florrie, that's what I say," said Nanny gamely. "She's studying Skakespeare and poetry and hist'ry."

"Well, there's brains," said Miss Dinsmore.

So, Nanny was proud of me. I paused by the tallboy.

Miss Dinsmore pressed on in a quiet, deadly way:

"I see Mrs Parrot's granddaughter, Edna, 'as a nice young chap – Elwyn – works for the municipal."

Edna Parrot had not finished grammar school. She'd gone to work at Steadman's Underwear on Oxford Street and suddenly become pretty, the way plain girls often did once they left school. I saw Nanny wince, and I wished then I had a nice-looking chap too, an Elwyn, if only for her sake. But what would I say to him?

"Wonderful what a bit of lipstick can do for a girl."

There was a tinkle of cups. I passed round the cakes. Miss Dinsmore changed the subject.

"And how are the new lodgers, Emmie?"

Nanny made a choking sound. She rented the small flat in the attic that had once been servants' quarters. The last lodger had been an old gentleman on the railway, Horace Pierce, "Hungry Horace", who had passed away in his sleep in the front bedroom upstairs. Recently, two old ladies, spinsters, a Miss Llewelyn and a Miss Vaughan had moved in.

"Dirty old lesbians!"

"No!" Miss Dinsmore's eyes glittered.

"You should have heard them yesterday morning, like a pair of old tomcats they were. I had to go up and bang on the door and separate them. And then they carried on outside on the pavement in front of the whole neighbourhood, yelling and spitting." It seemed Miss Vaughan had hit Miss Llewelyn on the head with her umbrella.

"Imagine," said Nanny. "Two women fighting like that over each other, jealous. Jealous of a *woman*."

Miss Dinsmore tutted and bit into a Welsh cake.

"Well, at least they pays their rent," said Nanny finally.

"Live and let live," agreed Miss Dinsmore, raising her glass. "*Iechyd da!* Tails up, Emmie!"

***

"You like sleeping with your Nanny, don't you, love?"

In the big front bedroom in the double, feather bed she'd shared with Granpa, a hushed sort of room with a deep bay window. A heavy dressing table with side mirrors swung back your reflection, startling, as if you shouldn't be there.

"Oh, can't I sleep in Davey's room this time?" My brother always had the small back bedroom when he stayed.

But of course I was there to keep Nanny company at night; my sister was always off with her boyfriend – she'd just left school and worked in an office. Besides, the back room wasn't aired.

Nanny's body would be bony hard as we lay side by side in the pressing dark. Sometimes in her sleep she'd fling a long thin arm over me, her body coming too close, her sagging breasts grazing, her breath sour in my face. Next morning she'd joke I was a bony one.

Later, upstairs, as I stood at the window in my nightie gazing out at the dark street, something tightened in my chest, looming. It was the sound of the sea far off at the bottom of the hill, thudding up the sands. I realised for the first time there was something about me I could not escape.

ONE DARK, RAINY, MISTY NIGHT

"Gigli or Caruso?"

Two famous tenors of my father's youth. He had dimmed the lights and put on a record, and I knew why. It was early evening and the front room was cast in a certain atmosphere, rainy light that fell through the front window which was draped in dark curtains. It gave off a hush that signalled our special time together, just Father and me.

Which one was singing the aria from *Turandot*? Caruso? He had a big deep voice, a soaring tenor. Gigli's voice was gentler, more lyrical. My face puckered; I struggled to give the right answer, the one he wanted. It was important, trying to remember what he'd always taught me: did the sound come from the stomach or the chest? Caruso's came from deep down, from the abdomen. No real daughter of his wouldn't know the difference by now. (I'd been able to tell the difference since I was seven, and now I was fifteen.) Father leaned forward on his elbows, legs apart, breathing heavily, waiting hopefully.

"Gigli, Daddy?"

"Nah!"

There was a thud followed by giggles from the adjoining room, separated from us by panelled French doors the local council had put in the council houses to give us a sense of being of the elite. Mother and Drusilla were holed up in there, smoking.

Father rapped on the panel, aggrieved. "Hey Mavis, pipe down will you, it's '*Nessun Dorma*', mun. *None Shall Sleep*."

"God, that's enough to bloody waken the dead! Here, have a cig, Dru."

More stifled giggles and a squeal. The sad strains of *"Nessun Dorma"* rose through the gloom. Rain nuzzled against the window, a pale mist over the houses opposite that hung like spectres, the distant trees ghost-like. Caruso's tenor voice rose. *"None shall sleep! None shall sleep! You too, princess, in your cold room watch the stars that tremble with love…"* Opera was all about crossed love, betrayals and mourning.

"God, how can Kezia *stand* it?" I could hear Drusilla hiss, her cigarette no doubt clenched between her teeth. "Talk about dreary. She can't know what any of it means – how could she? It's all in Italian." Drusilla herself listened to Radio Luxembourg on AM radio – *"Let's Go to the Hop!"* – *"Rock Around the Clock! We're gonna rock rock rock until the broad daylight…!"* – *"If you would only say you care…"* – She had a dinky portable radio her boyfriend gave her.

There was a clink of wine glasses, Mother and Drusilla having a good time together, a sip of cheap sherry Father wouldn't approve of; he neither smoked nor drank. (Sometimes, after Father left for work at the power station, if he was on night shift, which started at ten and ended at six the next morning, Mother would kick back the carpet as soon as he was out of the house. She'd get out an old dance record from the cabinet, the *Continental Tango*, or *Jealousy*. One two three – dip – turn – one two three – dip – I'd feel her body against me as we swung around the furniture, Mother leading. "It's only a bit of fun," she'd say. Sometimes she'd sneaked out with Mrs Atherly up the road – they were going off dancing in the Palais in town ("Don't tell your father, and keep the door locked, Davey will be with you." Our older brother, reading comics. "I won't be long" – more fun). I'd looked out the window anxiously, hiding behind the curtain and seen Mrs Atherly, whom Mother called Dolly, hurrying across the street through the mist with her youngest in her arms, wrapped in a blanket, and Jilly and Trevor Atherly following in their pyjamas. Trevor had been nine like me; he was in my class at school. Mrs Atherly was dropping them off at Mrs Gwynfor's for her to mind while she was out dancing somewhere, with our mother. Her husband Mr Atherly was on night shift that evening; he was a fireman. Mammy had giggled, flustered and excited. "It's only fun. Why shouldn't I have some fun?" She meant after the war, a terrifying time followed by rationing. Coupons for this, coupons for that. She loved the jazzy red dress she'd made herself. You had to seize the moment. She wanted laughter, admiration, drinks like rationed gin and tonic and – I now see clearly – temptation.

Father put on a bass for a change of pace (groans from behind the panelled doors). "My God, what next? Oh no! Chaliapin!" Another groan from Mother. "More like Charlie yappin'," she tittered. "Always sounds like he has a poker up his arse!"

Shrieks from Drusilla. "*Oh Ma, you're terrible!*" They collapsed laughing.

Feodor Chaliapin, greatest bass baritone in the world, according to the experts and Father; he was Russian.

"When did 'e die, Kezia?"

"1938, Daddy."

"Greatest *basso cantante*," said Father. Chaliapin's growly deep voice trembled through the living room and out into the dusky, damp night; he was singing "*Mashenka*". The flames leapt in the fire.

"And what was his greatest role?"

"Oh-h, um… Boris Gudenov."

"Very good, very good."

I was truly his daughter.

Father sighed and turned up the volume to block out the laughter from the dining room, which, of course, was spoiling the timbre. "Remember that, Kezia. 'Timbre' is the thing in a voice. You got to 'ave timbre, mun."

"Yes, Daddy."

Another favourite coming up. "You knows this one, Kezia." Giuseppe De Luca, baritone, singing with Amelita Galli-Curci and Caruso and others I forgot – there were six of them, six great voices of the century singing the great sextet *"Chi Mi Frena In Tal Momento?"* – *"What from vengeance now restrains me?"* (*"Who will stop me in this moment?"* Edgardo crying, *"I love you, heartless girl, I love you still!"*) Oh, I did love it how the voices moved in and out, balancing and challenging in wonderful counterpoint, tenors, baritone, sopranos, contralto, thrilling – and the way Galli-Curci soared on that one pure, terrible high note at the end that made everything shatter, and you're never the same again. For a moment, I forgot Father and how he always stared at me as I sat in the chair, my legs tight together. I kept my eyes averted, my face composed, conscious of him, how he seemed to know everything about me without a word said; of course he did. *Oh, what from vengeance now restrains me?* I shifted my gaze.

"*Lucia di Lammermoor*, Act eleven," he breathed. "January twenty-fifth, 1917." All of Father's records were valuable, original RCA recordings I was to inherit one day (the only child willing, otherwise they would end up in the dump). 78 RPMs, including a heavy, prized one-sided record that Drusilla said was enough to put your arms out of joint: Dame Clara Butt, contralto, singing "The Lost Chord" – "God, let's hope she never finds it!" Drusilla would raise her eyes drolly to the ceiling, and you couldn't help but laugh.

Dame Clara's voice boomed in a thrilling way: *"Seated one day at the organ, I was weary and ill at ease…"*

"No wonder," snorted Drusilla through the partition. "I'd be ill at ease too with a voice like that!" Clara Butt had been six feet tall and had a deep voice like a man's. "Abnormal, if you ask me." But it was a beautiful voice, deep and soothing.

Father looked at me intently, another test coming up. It was Caruso again, his all-time favourite, "voice of the century" he observed.

What had Puccini himself said of Caruso singing in *Manon*?

"He is singing like a god!" That one was easy.

"Right you are, Kezia. An' when was that?"

I hesitated. "Um. At the Met, 1907."

"Right again!" He looked impressed. What a daughter.

The bright coal fire gave off a rosy glow in the hot, small room, low-ceilinged, dim and close. Too close, the closeness I recoiled from, his male animal smell; but I'd not leave him alone with his records – it might break his heart, though I'd have loved to be in the other room with Mammy and Dru, screaming, laughing and having a tipple. He relied on me. How did he know the great arias when he could hardly read or write? (I was never quite sure about this.) Mother would scoff at him and his supposed "Italian".

"Oh but you don't need to know the meaning to appreciate the music, Mam," I'd ventured.

"See! Kezia knows." Father gave me a gratified look.

"Oh *her*."

She'd come in to the room to tell Daddy his butties were packed ready for night shift, and shouldn't he be leaving, it was after nine?

All that was long ago, at a time when people gathered after work around a coal fire on a long, damp, rainy, misty night to listen to opera. The old Victrola phonograph (later he got a Bush radiogram) with the iconic "His Master's Voice" trademark, a white dog looking into the trumpet, now an antique and probably priceless, going back to the 1940s, played 78 RPM singles. Father's thick, working-man's fingers would gently brush the vinyl record with a little velvet cushion – "Dust ruins a record" – before placing it on the turntable and carefully lowering the diamond-headed needle into the groove, for the magic to begin, the most revered of all his arias:

Pagliacci. Act II, "Vesti la Giubba" – *"On With the Motley".*
"On with the motley, and the paint, and the powder…
The world will cry 'Bravo'… a-ha ha ha ha ha…"

Father would bend forward in the chair, listening intently to Canio's lament as he discovers his wife's faithlessness. Canio putting on the smiling mask, donning his clown's costume ready for his performance – for the show must go on, life must go on! – though his heart was breaking.

… The silence that followed, the rain pressing against the panes… Could I ever forget Giuseppe di Stefano, Rosa Ponselle,

Renata Scotto, magical names lost in time, their vinyl records in the cardboard sleeves, now also priceless. Amelita Galli-Curci (adored coloratura of the opera world), singing "The Last Rose of Summer"? It was said her pure high notes could shatter a crystal chandelier. "Better put away the china, Mam," Drusilla would warn.

Giuseppe De Lucia sang at Caruso's funeral on 3 August 1921. The great tenor had died young, at forty-eight, of kidney failure. "It wuz them Egyptian cigarettes he smoked," growled Father. He had been only a boy at the time, but I think he mourned Caruso's passing for the rest of his life.

… Wistful hours on a damp, rainy, misty night in autumn by the fire, and the opening strains of a half-forgotten aria drifting through the window, not realising the moment, the love, could never return.

AUTHOR PROFILE

Granddaughter of a Welsh coal miner, Thelma Wheatley was born in Swansea and grew up in the Mumbles. She graduated from Aberystwyth University, then took a Master's Degree in English at York University, Toronto. She is an award-winning author of three books, one of which was inspired by her autistic son. *And Neither Have I Wings to Fly*, about the institutionalisation of the mentally handicapped in Canada, was shortlisted for the Wales Book of the Year Award, 2014, and also won Bronze Medal in Indie Awards. Thelma taught autistic children with special needs for many years in the Toronto area, and gave presentations on raising autistic children. She was a presenter on autism with AutismCymry, and gave talks in Swansea and Cardiff and at Aberystwyth University Theological College. She lives in Toronto, but also spends time in Swansea, in the Mumbles.

You can contact Thelma through her website:
www.thelmawheatley.com.

She is on LinkedIn, and on Facebook.

WHAT DID YOU THINK OF

LET'S GO PLAY IN THE BOMB BUILDINGS: A WELSH GIRLHOOD?

A big thank you for purchasing this book. It means a lot that you chose this book specifically from such a wide range on offer. I do hope you enjoyed it.

Book reviews are incredibly important for an author. All feedback helps them improve their writing for future projects and for developing this edition. If you are able to spare a few minutes to post a review on Amazon, that would be much appreciated.

Publisher Information

rowanvale
books

Rowanvale Books provides publishing services to independent authors, writers and poets all over the globe. We deliver a personal, honest and efficient service that allows authors to see their work published, while remaining in control of the process and retaining their creativity. By making publishing services available to authors in a cost-effective and ethical way, we at Rowanvale Books hope to ensure that the local, national and international community benefits from a steady stream of good quality literature.

For more information about us, our authors or our publications, please get in touch.

www.rowanvalebooks.com
info@rowanvalebooks.com